ARMENIA
in Pictures

VGS

Bella Waters

TF
CB
Twenty-First Century Books

Contents

Lerner Publishing Group, Inc. realizes that current information and statistics quickly become out of date. To extend the usefulness of the Visual Geography Series, we developed www.vgsbooks.com, a website offering links to up-to-date information, as well as in-depth material, on a wide variety of subjects. All of the websites listed on www.vgsbooks.com have been carefully selected by researchers at Lerner Publishing Group, Inc. However, Lerner Publishing Group, Inc. is not responsible for the accuracy or suitability of the material on any website other than www.lernerbooks.com. It is recommended that students using the Internet be supervised by a parent or teacher. Links on www.vgsbooks.com will be regularly reviewed and updated as needed.

Website address: www.lernerbooks.com

Twenty-First Century Books
A division of Lerner Publishing Group, Inc.
241 First Avenue North
Minneapolis, MN 55401 U.S.A.

web enhanced @ www.vgsbooks.com

Library of Congress Cataloging-in-Publication Data

Waters, Bella.
    Armenia in pictures / by Bella Waters.
      p. cm. – (Visual geography series)
    Includes bibliographical references and index.
    ISBN 978-0-8225-8576-3 (lib. bdg. : alk. paper)
     1. Armenia (Republic)–Juvenile literature. 2. Armenia (Republic)–Pictorial works–Juvenile literature.
I. Title.
DK685.6.D4 2009
947.56–dc22
                                                2007044784

Manufactured in the United States of America
1 2 3 4 5 6 – BP – 14 13 12 11 10 09

INTRODUCTION

Armenia is a small and ancient nation. It sits in the Caucasus region—a mountainous territory between the Black and Caspian seas. Through the centuries, large empires—Turkey to the west, Russia to the north, and many others—have attacked and sometimes conquered Armenian territory. Through it all, Armenia has managed to maintain its distinct culture and national pride.

People have lived in Armenia since prehistoric times. In about 10,000 B.C., Armenians settled down into farming villages. Armenia became a unified nation—with its own language, customs, government, and artwork.

The first large empire to conquer Armenia was Persia (modern-day Iran) in the 500s B.C. The Persians were followed by the Greeks and then the Romans. These early conquerors allowed the Armenians a certain amount of self-government and independence.

Armenia became a Christian nation in the early 300s A.D. It adopted its own alphabet one hundred years later. Both Christianity

and a written language helped Armenia strengthen its cultural and political identity. Armenian architects designed magnificent stone churches. Artists created lush illustrations for religious texts. Writers recorded Armenian history, folklore, and poetry.

Foreign nations continued to invade Armenia. By the 1700s, Armenia was split between two powerful groups—Russia and the Ottoman Empire, based in Turkey. The Turks proved to be cruel rulers. Armenians in Turkish territory suffered discrimination and brutality at the hands of Turkish authorities. The violence reached a crescendo during World War I (1914–1918), when the Turkish government systematically murdered about 1.5 million Armenian Turks. This genocide (the mass killing of an ethnic group) stands as the worst tragedy in Armenian history. It also strengthened Armenians' resolve to be a free and independent people.

For much of the twentieth century, Armenia was part of a nation called the Soviet Union. Once again, Armenians suffered under a

repressive government. In 1991 the Soviet Union broke apart, and Armenia declared its independence. It became a democratic republic.

The early years of independence were difficult. The reemerging nation coped with war with its neighbor Azerbaijan, a failing economy, and the aftermath of a devastating 1988 earthquake. The 1990s were stressful times, but gradually the economy improved. The political situation stabilized.

In the twenty-first century, Armenia has enjoyed strong economic growth. It is working with the international community to strengthen its financial and democratic institutions. Armenia has a large diaspora—a community of people who live outside the country but trace their ancestry to Armenia. This community has helped its homeland with critical moral and financial support.

Modern Armenia is home to about 3 million people. It is a land of many treasures. From its historic sites to its lively arts scene to its breathtaking mountain scenery, it has much to offer for both visitors and locals alike. After thousands of years of foreign rule and conflict, Armenians are finally in charge of their own destiny. They seem poised for prosperity and high achievement in the years to come.

THE LAND

Armenia covers an area of 11,506 square miles (29,800 square kilometers)—slightly larger than the U.S. state of Maryland. The country is shaped somewhat like a watering can, with a spout pointing to the southeast.

The nation of Turkey sits to the west of Armenia. Georgia sits to the north. On Armenia's eastern border is the nation of Azerbaijan and the disputed territory of Nagorno-Karabakh. Iran borders Armenia at the very south—right at the end of the watering can's spout. The small region of Naxcivan is cradled underneath the spout, on Armenia's southwestern border. Naxcivan is part of Azerbaijan, but it doesn't touch the rest of that nation. Armenia also contains three tiny regions called enclaves that lie entirely within Armenia but belong to Azerbaijan. Armenia owns its own enclave in western Azerbaijan.

Armenia is part of the Caucasus—the region between the Black and the Caspian seas in southwestern Asia. Armenia does not border either of the seas, however. It is a landlocked country, with no boundary on an ocean or a sea.

◉ Terrain

Armenia is very mountainous. Mountain ranges crisscross the country, with small plains and river valleys in between. The main ranges are the Dzhavakhet and Bazum in the northwest, the Shakhdag in the northeast, the Zangezur in the far south, the Geghama and Vardenis in the center of the nation, and the Armenian Highland in the west. Armenia's mountain ranges are all part of the Caucasus Mountains—a large mountain chain that runs between the Black and the Caspian seas. Many of Armenia's mountains are higher than 10,000 feet (3,000 meters). The highest point in the country is Mount Aragats in west central Armenia. It measures 13,418 feet (4,090 m) above sea level. The entire Caucasus range is prone to earthquakes.

Although mountains dominate, the nation has other geographical highlights. One of them is large Lake Sevan, near the Azerbaijan border. Another is the Ararat Plain, which stretches from west central Armenia southward into Turkey. This large plain is home to the

GEORGIA

UKRAINE RUSSIA ASIA
GEORGIA
Black Sea ARMENIA AZERBAIJAN Caspian Sea
TURKEY
Mediterranean Sea IRAQ IRAN
SAUDI
ARABIA Arabian
Peninsula
AFRICA Red Sea
Arabian
Sea
0 500 Miles
0 500 KM

C
A
U
C
A
S
U
S

Bazum Range
Debed
River
Agstev R.

Ozhavakhet
Range

Shakhdag Range

AZERBAIJAN

Mount
Aragats

Hrazdan River

Geghama Range

Lake
Sevan

M
O
U
N
T
A
I
N
S

ARARAT
PLAIN

Araks River

Vardenis Range

Nagorno-
Karabakh
[AZERBAIJAN]

ARMENIAN

Arpa River

Ughtasar
Mountain

Mount
Ararat

HIGHLAND

Zangezur Range

TURKEY

Naxcivan
[AZERBAIJAN]

IRAN

Armenia

Feet	Meters	
9843	3000	Mountains
6562	2000	Uplands
3281	1000	Lowlands
1640	500	

Elevation

N

▲ Mountain peak

0   25 Miles

0   25 KM

Mount Ararat rises above the Araks River, which defines the border between Armenia and Turkey.

nation's capital, Yerevan, as well as other cities and farms.

Lakes and Rivers

Lake Sevan is Armenia's only large lake. Covering about 5 percent of the country's territory, it nestles between the Shakhdag, Vardenis, and Geghama mountain ranges in east central Armenia. Armenia has about a hundred other lakes, all of them very small.

Many rivers flow down from the mountains of Armenia. The Araks River, the country's longest waterway, forms part of Armenia's border with Turkey and Iran. Several other big rivers drain into the Araks. These include the Hrazdan, which flows out of Lake Sevan, and the Arpa, which crosses the country south of the Vardenis Range. Other Armenian rivers, such as the Debed and the Agstev, flow eastward into Azerbaijan. Armenia's rivers flow fast year-round, especially when the snow melts in spring. The rivers tumble over many rapids and waterfalls as they rush down from the mountains.

THE POWER OF ARARAT

Mount Ararat is not in modern Armenia, but Armenians look to this mountain as their spiritual center. According to the Bible, after a massive flood, Noah's ark came to rest on the top of Mount Ararat. Noah's sons and descendants then settled throughout the Ararat Plain and created the ancient kingdom of Armenia. In modern times, Mount Ararat is part of Turkey. But it is visible from Yerevan and still serves as a symbol of the glory of historic Armenia.

The **Ararat Plain** is one of the sunniest places in the world. It gets about 2,700 hours of sunshine each year.

Climate

Armenia has cold winters and hot summers, with mild weather in spring and fall. Temperatures vary by elevation—with the warmest readings in the plains and valleys and colder readings in the mountains. In January, temperatures average about 23°F (−5°C) on the Ararat Plain and about 10°F (−12°C) in the mountains. Sometimes, frigid air sweeps in from the north in winter, and temperatures drop well below freezing.

In July and August, 77°F (25°C) is the average temperature for the Ararat Plain. In the mountains, the average is about 50°F (10°C) in July and August.

Armenians enjoy more than three hundred sunny days each year. Rainfall is low. It varies from 8 to 16 inches (20 to 40 centimeters) per year on the plains to 32 inches (81 cm) per year in the mountains. Snow falls mainly from December to February, but many of Armenia's mountain peaks are covered in snow year-round.

FIRST FOODS

Scientists believe that apricots originated in Armenia. At Armenian excavation sites, archaeologists have found apricot pits dating from six thousand years ago. Scientists also think that about ten thousand years ago, Armenian farmers were the first people to grow wheat.

Flora and Fauna

Armenia's plant life changes with elevation. Low-lying plains are covered with sagebrush, juniper, honeysuckle, and other shrubs and small trees. These are plants that can survive without much moisture. At middle elevations, as the land grows hillier, the main plants are short grasses and thorny bushes.

As the land climbs even higher, at about 7,000 feet (2,133 m) above sea level, trees begin to cover the landscape. In the north, beech forests are common. In the south, oak trees predominate. Pistachio, almond, honeysuckle, maple, and dogwood trees also grow on mountain slopes. Larch, pine, and spruce trees grow at higher elevations.

Above the forest zone, at about 8,000 feet (2,438 m), plant life becomes sparse. Only short grasses grow on the rocky mountain slopes. On the highest peaks, the landscape is almost bare, with only small, cold-resistant plants growing among the rocks.

Different animals also live at different altitudes. Boars and jackals (wild dogs) live in Armenia's low-lying areas. Snakes, lizards, and scorpions live there too. Higher up, on the forested mountain slopes, wildcats, lynxes, and squirrels make their homes. Big, brown Syrian bears also live in mountain forests. Higher mountain slopes provide good grazing land for mountain goats and sheep.

Birds are found in great numbers in Armenia. Woodcocks, robins, nuthatches, warblers, and woodpeckers live in mountain forests. Eagles, ospreys, vultures, buzzards, and falcons make homes higher up in the mountains. Pelicans, cranes, and other water-loving birds live around Lake Sevan.

Lake Sevan, as well as the nation's many rivers, provides a home for carp, trout, chub, whitefish, salmon, and other kinds of fish. Many of these fish are not native to Armenia but have been introduced from other places.

BIG BIRD

The lammergeyer, which makes its home in the Armenian mountains, has a wingspan between 9 and 10 feet (2.7 and 3 m). This big bird is sometimes called the bearded vulture because it has black feathers around its mouth. It has an orange neck and breast, with a black tail and wings. Lammergeyers feed on wounded, sick, and dead animals.

Natural Resources

Armenia's resources include many mineral deposits. Large copper deposits are located near the city of Kajaran in the south. Molybdenum, a strong, silvery-white metal, is also mined at Kajaran. The city of Zod, southeast of Lake Sevan, has gold mines. Lead, zinc, silver, bauxite, marble, granite, and other minerals are also found in Armenia.

One of Armenia's most valuable resources is its rushing rivers. On the Hrazdan and other rivers, Armenians have built hydroelectric stations. These plants harness the power of moving water to generate electricity. About one-third of Armenia's electric power comes from its hydroelectric plants.

About one-fifth of Armenia's land is arable, or suitable for farming. The soil is very fertile, but because of low rainfall, farmers must irrigate (artificially water) their fields. The nation's major crops are fruits, grains, and vegetables.

Environmental Problems

Armenia suffers from environmental problems common to many industrialized nations. In the cities, factories, cars, and power plants pollute the air and water. The Metsamor nuclear power plant near

The **Metsamor nuclear power plant** was closed after an earthquake in 1988 but reopened in the late 1990s.

Yerevan is particularly hazardous. Experts say the plant is not well built. In the event of an earthquake, the plant could break down and spread deadly radiation into the atmosphere.

In rural areas, farmers use fertilizers and pesticides. These chemicals run off into rivers and lakes, harming the plants and animals that live there. Mining operations also pollute the surrounding land, lakes, and rivers.

Many of Armenia's forests have been cut down for firewood. When the trees are cut, smaller plants and animals can no longer make their homes there. Many animals in Armenia are endangered. This means their numbers have dwindled and they are in danger of dying out altogether. These species include the mouflon, a type of wild sheep; the Persian ibex, or wild goat; and the Persian leopard.

Lake Sevan is another area of concern. In the mid-twentieth century, to power hydroelectric stations and to irrigate farmland, Armenians drew large amounts of water from the Hrazdan River, which is fed by Lake Sevan. As a result, the lake steadily drained. By 2001 it had fallen from a height of 6,319 feet (1,915 m) above sea level to 6,257 feet (1,896 m). The falling water level, combined with pollution, hurt plant and animal life in and around the lake. The Sevan trout, which once lived in the lake in large numbers, had almost completely died out by the early 2000s. To protect the lake and its plants and animals, engineers have reduced the amount of water taken from the Hrazdan River. As a result, the lake level has begun to rise slightly.

The **Armenian mouflon** is thought to be one of two ancestors of all modern sheep breeds.

Two churches overlook **Lake Sevan and the town of Sevan** on the far shore. The churches once served the monastery (religious complex) of Sevanavank, founded there in A.D. 874.

To protect its remaining wild places, Armenia has set aside about 12 percent of its land as national parks and preserves. The largest park is Sevan National Park, which surrounds the lake. Other big parks are the Khosrov Nature Reserve, the Dilijan Nature Reserve, and the Shikahogh Nature Reserve. These parks provide safe homes for wildlife. They are off limits to building, hunting, and other human activities. The government has also established a Ministry of Nature Protection. This agency has passed laws to limit air and water pollution and to strengthen environmental protection.

Cities

YEREVAN (population 1.1 million) is Armenia's capital city. It is also the biggest city in Armenia. Yerevan is home to about one-third of the nation's people. It is situated along the Hrazdan River on the fertile Ararat Plain. From Yerevan, residents can see Mount Ararat, which sits in Turkish territory but serves as a spiritual symbol for all Armenians.

Yerevan traces its founding to 782 B.C., when King Argishti I built a fortress on the site. The fortress soon became a thriving town. Over many centuries, the city grew and changed, until an earthquake flattened it completely in 1679. Afterward, Yerevan's residents rebuilt their city. It fell to Russian conquerors in 1827.

In 1918 Armenians declared their nation to be an independent republic, with Yerevan as its capital. The republic was short-lived—the Soviet Union soon took over Armenia. But Yerevan remained the capital of Soviet Armenia. Soviet leaders remade the city according to a master plan—with a grand central square, broad tree-lined avenues, and impressive public buildings. During the Soviet era, the city grew to be thirty times its former size. People flooded in from the countryside to take jobs in the city. To house them, city planners erected block upon block of bleak, boxy, concrete apartment buildings.

Modern Yerevan is Armenia's cultural and educational center. It has churches, museums, theaters, libraries, and colleges. It is also the center of the nation's government and business. Visitors here will find bustling streets filled with cars and pedestrians, as well as office towers, restaurants, and Internet cafés.

Apartment buildings line the **skyline of Yerevan.** Soviet planners modernized the city during the twentieth century, destroying many historical buildings.

EARTHQUAKE ZONE

Earth's crust, or outer shell, is made up of about thirty tectonic plates. These gigantic slabs of rock move slowly and sometimes collide with each other. Earthquakes occur when two plates collide. Armenia sits on a line where the Arabian Plate meets the larger Eurasian Plate. Armenia has suffered many earthquakes from the collision of these plates. The most recent big quake occurred in December 1988.

Rescue teams search for survivors after an earthquake destroyed the city of Gyumri (then Leninakan) in 1988.

GYUMRI (population 150,000), located in the northwest, is Armenia's second-largest city. Like Yerevan, the city dates to ancient times. It was an important city during the many centuries of foreign rule in Armenia. Russia took over the city in the 1830s and renamed it Alexandropol, after the wife of the Russian czar (emperor). During the Soviet era, the named changed to Leninakan, after Vladimir Lenin, the first leader of the Soviet Union.

On December 7, 1988, a massive earthquake hit northwestern Armenia. The quake killed 25,000 people and left 500,000 homeless. In Gyumri (then called Leninakan), about 60 percent of the buildings were flattened. Three years later, the Soviet Union broke apart, and Leninakan took back its original name, Gyumri.

Rebuilding Gyumri after the earthquake was a long, slow process. With their homes destroyed, many people lived in old metal shipping containers. Even in 2008, twenty years after the quake, the city still contains piles of rubble, abandoned buildings, and makeshift housing. Modern Gyumri is an industrial center, with textile factories and copper-processing plants. It has some interesting old churches but few other cultural attractions.

Visit www.vgsbooks.com for links to websites with additional information about the cities in Armenia. Visit Yerevan's City Hall and view pictures of the famous churches of Vagharshapat. Get city maps and learn about traveling to Armenia.

VANADZOR (population 100,000) sits in the center of northern Armenia, on the Debed River. It, too, is an ancient city with thousands of years of history. Like other Armenian cities, its name has changed over the years. It was once called Kharaklisa, which means "black church," and then Kirovakan (after a Soviet leader) during Soviet times. The modern name, Vanadzor, comes from the nearby Vanadzor River.

The 1988 earthquake, centered to the west, did slight damage to Vanadzor. But most of the city survived intact. Like Gyumri, Vanadzor is an industrial city. A huge chemical plant provides jobs for many residents.

VAGHARSHAPAT (population 50,000), formerly called Ejmiadzin, is a fascinating city west of Yerevan. The city is the headquarters of the Armenian Apostolic Church. According to legend, in the fourth century A.D., a holy man named Gregory saw a vision of Jesus striking a golden hammer there. Shortly after his vision, Gregory established a monastery, or a religious complex, at this site. Modern-day visitors come to Vagharshapat to see the monastery, as well as several historic churches.

HISTORY AND GOVERNMENT

People have lived in Armenia since prehistoric times. On the slopes of Mount Aragats, archaeologists have found crude stone tools dating from more than 600,000 years ago. Prehistoric Armenians were hunter-gatherers. They got their food by hunting, fishing, and gathering wild plants. They probably traveled from place to place, looking for game animals and other food supplies.

In about 10,000 B.C., Armenians began to farm. People settled down into farming villages. They grew crops such as wheat and barley. They also raised livestock, including goats, sheep, and cattle. These animals provided people with meat, milk, wool, and skins. People of this era learned new technologies, such as metalworking. They made tools and vessels out of copper, bronze, and iron. They also made clay pots. They learned to weave wool into rugs, clothing, and other textiles.

Historians think that Armenians of this era worshipped the Sun and other heavenly bodies. Ancient Armenian rock carvings show images of the Sun, the Moon, and the stars. Archaeologists have found

stone monuments that people might have used to track the movements of the Sun and the Moon.

◉ The First Kingdom

Armenian society continued to grow more complex. New groups moved into the region from surrounding territories. People spoke many different languages, depending on where they lived. They worshipped different gods. They lived in small tribes, or family groups, but had no central ruler.

In the 1300s B.C., several tribes joined together to create Armenia's first kingdom. This was the kingdom of Urartu. It was centered at Lake Van, in modern-day Turkey. At its peak, Urartu controlled all of present-day Armenia and much of present-day Turkey. Urartu's rulers built palaces, fortresses, temples, and roads throughout their empire. They maintained an army to protect their territory and to fight enemies.

In the 600s B.C., a new group moved to Urartu from the west. These

THE LAND OF HAIK

The name Armenia has been in use since the 500s B.C. It first appeared in an inscription carved into a rock in ancient Persia. The name might come from a legendary Armenian leader named Aram. But Armenians also have another name for their homeland. They call it Hayastan, or "the Land of Haik." According to legend, Haik was a great-great-grandson of Noah. Legends say that he was a heroic warrior, who slew an Assyrian tyrant on the shores of Lake Van. Stories also say that Haik was 130 years old when he killed the tyrant, that he died at age 400, and that he had three hundred sons. Although Haik's story is clouded in myth, Armenians nevertheless look upon him as the father of their nation.

people intermarried and mixed in with the local population. The newcomers also brought a new language to Urartu. This language spread throughout the kingdom. It became the basis for modern-day Armenian.

Between Great Empires

In the 500s B.C., people called the Medes conquered Urartu. Soon afterward, the Medes fell to the Persians, a large and powerful empire to the southwest. Thus the people of Armenia became part of the Persian Empire. By then, Armenia had a distinct identity, with its own language and culture.

The Persians gave Armenia a degree of independence. They allowed a local leader to rule Armenia. But the Armenians had to pay taxes to the Persians, in the form of horses.

The Persians introduced a new religion to Armenia: Zoroastrianism. This religion teaches that a supreme god created the world. It also teaches that Earth is a battleground between good and evil spirits.

In 331 B.C., the Greek general Alexander the Great conquered Persia, bringing Armenia into his empire. Like the rulers of Persia, Alexander allowed the Armenians a certain amount of independence. After Alexander's death in 323 B.C., local kings continued to rule in Armenia.

An Armenian artist of the fourteenth century painted this illustration for a story about **Alexander the Great** *(wearing red cloak).*

In 95 B.C., a ruler named Tigranes came to power in Armenia. Called Tigranes the Great, he conquered new territory and created the Armenian Empire. It extended from the Mediterranean Sea in the south to present-day Georgia in the north.

The new empire did not last long. After Tigranes's death, his son Artavasdes ruled Armenia. In 36 B.C. he surrendered his territory to the powerful Roman Empire, based in modern-day Italy. The Romans, like the Persians and the Greeks, gave Armenia a certain measure of independence. The Roman emperor allowed local kings to rule in Armenia. For a brief period, Persia took over Armenia again in the late A.D. 200s. But Rome defeated the Persians in 298, and Armenia returned to the Roman fold.

Cultural Foundations

By this time, a new religion—Christianity—was spreading throughout the Roman Empire. In the early centuries A.D., the religion had started to take hold in Armenia. Its biggest champion was a nobleman named Gregory. According to legend, Gregory was a holy man who performed miracles. He was later called Saint Gregory the Illuminator (Illustrator).

In either 301 or 314 (most historians accept the later date), Gregory baptized Tiridates III, the Armenian king, as a Christian. Tiridates then made Christianity the official religion of Armenia. It was the first nation to formally adopt Christianity.

The adoption of Christianity was a turning point for Armenia. The religion further solidified

Saint Gregory the Illuminator baptizes King Tiridates III, in this Italian painting from the 1700s.

Armenians into a unified nation and helped set them apart from their non-Christian neighbors. The religion also served as a basis for future Armenian literature, music, art, and architecture.

About one hundred years later, Armenians embraced another invention. It, too, helped unify the nation's identity and culture. This invention was a new alphabet, created by a cleric named Mesrob in the early 400s. The alphabet contains thirty-eight letters. Mesrob designed the alphabet so that Armenians could write the Bible and other religious works in their own language. (Previously, educated Armenians had written in Greek, Latin, and other languages.)

The new alphabet helped strengthen the influence of Christianity in Armenia. In addition to religious writings, scholars used the alphabet to translate scientific and medical texts into Armenian from Greek and Latin. They also used it to create new literary works.

New Rulers

Also in the early 400s, the Romans made a deal with the Persians. The two empires decided to split Armenia between them and remove the Armenian king from power. Under the agreement, a small portion of eastern Armenia remained with the Eastern Roman Empire, later called the Byzantine Empire. The bulk of Armenia went to the Persians.

The Persians ordered the Armenians in their territory to convert to Zoroastrianism. By then, Christianity was a powerful force in Armenian society. Outraged by the attack on their faith, the Armenians revolted against Persia. A church leader named Vardan Mamikonian led a small Armenian force against the much larger Persian army. The two sides clashed at the Battle of Avarayr in 451. The Armenians were badly beaten, but they

In this 1569 Armenian painting, a small Armenian force *(at bottom)* attacks Persian warriors at the **Battle of Avarayr.**

declared the battle a moral victory for Christianity. They continued to rebel throughout the following decades. Finally, to gain peace, the Persians gave the Armenians religious freedom.

In the 600s, another new religion came on the scene. This religion was Islam. Its adherents are called Muslims. Islam had begun on the Arabian Peninsula in present-day Saudi Arabia. It quickly spread throughout southwestern Asia and the Middle East. A Muslim army invaded Armenia in about 640 and won a decisive victory.

Muslim rulers tried to force the Armenians to accept Islam. They imprisoned Armenian religious leaders, destroyed Christian images, and taxed the Armenians heavily. To escape the oppression, some Armenians left their nation for Byzantine-held Armenia. Other Armenians rebelled against the Muslims. The conflict continued on and off for more than one hundred years. Finally, in 885, Muslim rulers backed off and agreed to let a local Christian king rule Armenia. That king was Ashot I. His reign ushered in a period of peace, artistic growth, and literary activity. Under Ashot and the kings who followed, Armenians built magnificent churches and created beautiful illuminated (illustrated) manuscripts.

Turks and Russians

The period of peace, religious freedom, and creativity did not last long. In the 1000s, an Islamic group called the Seljuk Turks attacked Armenia. The Seljuk Turks came from central Asia, east of the Caspian Sea. They defeated the Armenians at the Battle of Manzikert in 1071.

The Seljuk Turks were violent, repressive rulers. Under Seljuk control, Armenia's culture and economy declined. Once again, to escape oppression, some Armenians left their homeland for other places, including the Middle East and Europe.

There was one bright spot for the Armenians during this era, however. South of Seljuk territory, a new Armenian kingdom formed in 1080 in Cilicia, along the northern shore of the Mediterranean Sea. The Cilician Armenians produced great works of art and literature. They also allied with European knights called Crusaders. The Crusaders were Christians. They wanted to recapture the Middle East—the birthplace of Christianity, as well as Islam—from Muslim control. The Crusaders, and their Cilician allies, were unsuccessful in this quest. Despite numerous Crusades, Muslim forces continued to maintain power in the Middle East.

In the 1200s and 1300s, Armenia fell to new conquerors—first the Mongols (from Asia) and then the Mamluks (from Egypt). In the 1400s, the Ottoman Turks came to power. The Ottomans were Muslims from Turkey. They conquered a vast territory in the Middle East, eastern Europe, and the Caucuses.

The Persian emperor **Shah Abbas I** conquered Yerevan and other Armenian cities in 1620. He was known for his tolerance of Christians in his Islamic empire but also for his ruthlessness in battle.

The Ottoman Turks fought with the Persians for control of Armenia. In 1639 Armenia was again split, with the Ottomans taking the western portion and the Persians again taking the east. As before, some Armenians left their homeland rather than suffer at the hands of foreign conquerors. They moved to new homes in Europe, the Middle East, and as far away as India.

The Persian–Ottoman rivalry continued into the 1700s, until the two empires began to weaken. Their decline allowed a new force—the powerful Russian Empire—to expand its territory. The Russians pushed southward into the Caucasus and took over parts of Georgia, Azerbaijan, and Armenia. By the 1720s, Persia had lost most of its Armenian territory to Russia.

In the 1700s and 1800s, Armenians living under Russian rule enjoyed a fair amount of peace and prosperity. The Russians and the Armenians held some things in common, most notably the practice of Christianity. The Armenians felt a connection to the Russians as well as to the Christian nations of Europe.

Terror

Meanwhile, the Ottoman Turks retained control in western Armenia. The Turks allowed the Armenians to practice Christianity. But Turkish rule was harsh. Turkish sultans (rulers) taxed Armenians heavily. Armenians were not allowed to testify in court or carry weapons for self-defense. Despite the oppression, many Turkish Armenians managed to succeed in business and other professions. In fact, by the mid-1800s, Armenians controlled some of the most successful banks and businesses in the Ottoman Empire. They were also leaders in music and the arts.

Gradually, the treatment of Armenians in Turkey grew more and more violent. Turkish soldiers began to terrorize and kill Armenian villagers. Some Armenians fled eastward into Russian-held lands. Others appealed to the nations of Europe for help. Armenians also began to form political parties to fight for Armenian self-government within Turkish territory.

Turkish officials were alarmed. They saw the Armenian political parties as a dangerous, foreign threat to Turkish society. They began to crack down on Armenians even harder. Between 1894 and 1896, the Turkish government ordered the massacre of 300,000 Armenians.

In 1908 a group called the Young Turks came to power in Turkey. At first, the Young Turks promised fair treatment for Armenians and other ethnic groups. But they soon changed their policy. They began to argue that Turkey should be entirely Turkish and entirely Islamic. The persecution of Armenians in Turkey grew more and more harsh.

Soon afterward World War I (1914–1918) broke out in Europe. The war pitted Russia, France, and Great Britain against Germany and the Turks. When war arrived, Turkish rulers said that the Armenians were a bigger threat than ever. They argued that Christian Armenians would naturally ally themselves with the Christian, European powers at war with Turkey. This argument did not reflect the truth, however. In fact, most Armenians in Turkey did not rebel or show disloyalty to their rulers during the war. Thousands of Armenian men served obediently as soldiers in the Turkish army.

In the **Adana massacre of 1909,** Turkish soldiers joined a mob that murdered as many as thirty thousand Armenians in the city of Adana in southern Turkey.

Nevertheless, the Turks began a massive program to wipe out Armenians in Ottoman-held territory. In the spring of 1915, Turkish soldiers marched into Armenian villages and rounded up villagers of all ages. The soldiers shot or bayoneted some of the men immediately. They imprisoned and tortured others. The soldiers then herded up the remaining villagers. In some cases, they loaded these captives onto boats and then threw them overboard into lakes and rivers to drown. Most of the victims, however, were marched to the Syrian Desert and other wilderness areas. Along the way, Turkish soldiers robbed, raped, and beat the captives. Sick, weak, and hungry, many thousands died by the roadside. When they reached the desert, they were either massacred or left to die of thirst and starvation.

Historians believe that the Turks killed about 1.5 million Armenians during World War I. Some Armenians were able to escape the genocide. They fled from the Ottoman Empire to Russian-held Armenia, Europe, the United States, and other places. Others agreed to convert to Islam, thereby saving their lives.

Crossroads

As World War I raged, Russia fell into turmoil. In late 1917, a group of revolutionaries overthrew the czarist government. The revolutionaries were communists. They wanted to create a new kind of society. This society had no private businesses or private property. The government controlled the economy, and everyone shared equally in the nation's riches. The new communist leaders pulled Russia out of World War I. They set out to impose communism in all Russian-held territories. But the communists met with opposition. For several years, Russia endured a civil war as communist and noncommunist forces battled for control.

Since they were no longer fighting the Turks, Russian troops left the Caucasus. With the Russians gone, the Armenians saw a chance to set up their own government. After repelling several Turkish attacks, in 1918 the Armenians declared their nation to be an independent republic. The new nation included all of present-day Armenia and small portions of eastern Turkey.

World War I ended in late 1918 with a German and Turkish defeat. The Armenians hoped that the victorious nations of Europe (as well as the United States, which had entered the war in 1917) would support their young republic. But the nation was on shaky ground. It was filled with hungry refugees from the massacres in Turkey. The government was poor and weak. The international community did not send any soldiers to help the Armenians.

Meanwhile, by 1920 the Russian communists had consolidated their power. At the same time, the Turks had regrouped under the leadership of a man named Kemal Ataturk. Both the Russians and the Turks again advanced on Armenia. Once again, Armenia was caught between the ambitions of two powerful nations. Seeing the Russians as the lesser of two evils, Armenia surrendered to the new communist government in Russia. Yet again, many Armenians chose to leave their nation rather than live under foreign rule. Large numbers of Armenians moved to France and the United States.

A New Start

In 1922 Russia's leaders created a new nation—the Union of Soviet Socialist Republics, or the Soviet Union. At first, the Soviet government grouped Armenia, Georgia, and Azerbaijan together into one political unit. It was called the Transcaucasian Soviet Federated Socialist Republic. Yerevan was its capital city.

Soviet leaders devised a master plan for their new nation. They wanted to create a modern, industrialized economy throughout the Soviet Union. As part of this plan, Soviet engineers built irrigation systems, hydroelectric power plants, and factories throughout the Caucasus. Soviet leaders also combined thousands of small farms into gigantic, government-run farms.

Yerevan became a prominent city during this period. Yerevan State University, founded in 1920, underwent expansion. The Soviets also created new industries and founded new schools and libraries in the city. In the mid-1920s, the city was rebuilt according to a design by

Armenians pick cotton on a government-run farm during the Soviet era.

Armenian architect Alexander Tamanian. The centerpiece of the new Yerevan was the massive Republic Square, surrounded by grand public buildings and broad avenues. People began to flood into the city to work in government offices and other businesses. Some Armenians who had left their nation in the late nineteenth or early twentieth century returned from abroad to live in Yerevan and take part in the city's rich cultural and intellectual life.

In 1936, as part of a new Soviet constitution, Armenia, Georgia, and Azerbaijan were separated into individual republics. The new Armenian Soviet Socialist Republic had the same borders as present-day Armenia. It was the smallest of the fifteen Soviet republics.

Despair

At first, Armenia seemed to prosper under Soviet rule. But the communist government soon showed itself to be oppressive and corrupt. Under the Soviet system, the government told everyone where to live and where to work. People were not allowed to vote for their leaders. There was no freedom of the press or freedom of speech.

In the 1930s, a man named Joseph Stalin came to power in the Soviet Union. Stalin was a brutal dictator. He was also extremely paranoid. He believed that even his loyal followers were plotting against him. Between 1934 and 1939, Stalin attempted to purge, or rid, the Soviet Union of anyone who might threaten his power. He had

Soviet leader Joseph Stalin meets with women delegates from an Armenian workers' group.

Heavy machinery runs at a factory in Yerevan that specialized in making steel products.

millions of Soviet citizens arrested, imprisoned, and killed. At least 100,000 Armenians lost their lives in Stalin's purges.

Stalin also attacked the Christian Church, believing that it, too, was a threat to his power. In the 1930s, the Soviet government shut down nearly every church in Armenia and murdered church leaders. Devout Armenians had to worship in secret.

The Soviet Union fought in World War II (1939–1945) on the side of the Allies (including Great Britain and the United States). Although the battle lines never reached Armenia, about 630,000 Armenians served in the Soviet military during the conflict. About half of these soldiers died in the war. The war ended with an Allied victory.

◉ Poised for Change

After the war, industrialization continued in Armenia. The Soviet government set up huge factories in Yerevan, Gyumri (then called Leninakan), and Vanadzor (then called Kirovakan). These factories produced chemicals, farm equipment, vehicles, machinery, textiles, and consumer goods. Yerevan's population swelled, from about 50,000 people in the 1930s to 1.3 million after the war.

In some ways, Armenians prospered in the postwar era. The Soviet Union ran a system of high-quality schools and universities. The Armenians emerged from this system highly literate (able to read and write), well educated, and professionally accomplished. Many of them became officials in the Armenian communist government. Others held high-level jobs in agriculture and industry. Also during the postwar era, the Soviet government loosened restrictions on religious worship, and some Armenian churches reopened.

But repression continued. People who criticized the Soviet government still faced harsh punishment. Many Armenians—especially artists and intellectuals—fled to the West (western Europe and North America), where people enjoyed freedom of speech and freedom of the press.

In the 1960s and 1970s, the Soviet economic system began to crumble. Government-run farms were not able to produce enough food for the entire nation. Government-run factories grew run-down and outdated. Finally, Soviet citizens began to demand change. They wanted a free and open society, where people could speak their minds, run their own businesses, vote for their own leaders, and buy nice cars, homes, and other consumer products.

In Armenia, people also recalled their nation's long, proud history. Many Armenians hoped they could once again break free from foreign rule and establish an independent, democratic nation.

THE ARMENIAN DIASPORA

An estimated 4 to 10 million people of Armenian origin live in places outside Armenia—as far away as India, Australia, Argentina, and Canada. They are members of the Armenian diaspora. Diaspora—from a Greek word that means "disperse"—refers to an ethnic group whose members have spread out far from their ancestral homeland.

Many members of the Armenian diaspora maintain close family and spiritual ties to Armenia. Many give money to charities that help Armenia, or they send money to their relatives who still live there. After the 1988 earthquake, the Armenian diaspora contributed millions of dollars in relief.

In 2007 the Armenian parliament (legislature) passed a law allowing people of Armenian descent to get dual citizenship. In this way, members of the diaspora can become official Armenian citizens while still remaining citizens of the countries where they make their homes.

Crisis and Rebirth

In the 1980s, a number of events converged to change the course of Armenian history. First, in 1985, a new leader came to power in the Soviet Union. He was Mikhail Gorbachev. Gorbachev was a reformer. He saw that the Soviet economy was broken and needed to change. He introduced a policy called perestroika, or "restructuring." Under perestroika, the Soviet government loosened its control over the economy. For the first time, people in the Soviet Union could run their own small businesses. For the first time, they were allowed to form noncommunist political parties. Gorbachev introduced a second policy called glasnost, or "openness." This policy allowed Soviet citizens to express their political views more freely, without fear of being punished by the government.

Gorbachev's changes were welcome news in Armenia. Armenian people began to organize political parties. They talked again about creating an Armenian nation. As part of this movement, Armenia wanted to unite with the territory of Nagorno-Karabakh. This territory was officially part of Azerbaijan but was home to many Armenians.

In 1988 Armenia and Azerbaijan began to fight over control of Nagorno-Karabakh. In the course of the fighting, many civilians were killed on both sides. To escape the violence, hundreds of thousands of Armenians living in Azerbaijan fled to Armenia. Hundreds of thousands of Azeris (people of Azerbaijani ethnicity) living in Armenia fled to Azerbaijan. Creating even more chaos, a massive earthquake hit northwestern Armenia in late 1988, killing thousands and leaving many more homeless.

While Armenia coped with war and the aftermath of the 1988 quake, the Soviet Union was falling apart. The Soviet republics began defying the central Soviet government. Armenia, too, was ready to break free. In 1990 a group called the Armenian Pannational Movement took over the Armenian government and declared independence from the Soviet Union. On September 21, 1991, Armenian citizens officially voted in favor of independence. In October, Armenians went to the polls again and elected Levon Ter-Petrossian as their new president.

> The status of Nagorno-Karabakh is still uncertain. In 1991 Nagorno-Karabakh declared itself to be an independent republic. But the international community does not recognize its independence. International bodies say the territory is still part of Azerbaijan.

◉ Starting from Scratch

The Armenians soon learned that creating a new country would not be easy. For one thing, they were still at war with Azerbaijan over control of Nagorno-Karabakh. For another thing, the 1988 earthquake had massively damaged Gyumri, one of the Armenia's biggest cities. Even several years after the quake, the city was a disaster zone, and thousands of its residents were homeless.

Prior to the earthquake, Armenia had gotten much of its electrical power from the Metsamor nuclear plant west of Yerevan. But Armenians were worried. They knew that another earthquake might damage the plant—and spread deadly radiation into the atmosphere. To be safe, Armenian leaders shut down the plant. The shutdown greatly reduced Armenia's power supply.

Making matters worse, Azerbaijan and its ally Turkey imposed an economic blockade against Armenia. That meant that Armenia could not import energy, food, or other products from these neighbors. All at once, Armenia was drastically short on food and fuel. Its economy fell into shambles. Inflation, or rising prices, skyrocketed. Hundreds of thousands were homeless—either victims of the 1988 earthquake or Armenian refugees from Azerbaijan. People were poor, cold, hungry, and unemployed. In Yerevan, residents cut down the city's trees to burn as firewood. Hundreds of thousands moved to Russia, where prospects seemed brighter.

Gradually, Armenia began to put itself together. It adopted a new flag and created a new system of currency (money). It joined the United Nations and other international groups. It also joined the Commonwealth of Independent States—an association of former Soviet republics. In 1994 Armenia and Azerbaijan declared a cease-fire in the Nagorno-Karabakh conflict, but not before 25,000 fighters had been killed on both sides. In July 1995, Armenian voters approved a new national constitution.

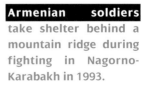

Armenian soldiers take shelter behind a mountain ridge during fighting in Nagorno-Karabakh in 1993.

Anxious citizens crowd around a baker's window during the early 1990s, when food was scarce in Armenia.

Armenians began to open private businesses. Farms, apartment houses, and factories that had been government owned and operated during the Soviet era converted to private ownership. The economy steadily improved. And despite worries about earthquakes, the government reopened the Metsamor nuclear plant, thereby increasing the nation's energy supply.

But the situation was rocky at best. Politicians of various parties accused one another of crime, corruption, and election fraud. The chaos came to a head in 1999, when five gunmen stormed into a meeting of Armenia's parliament, or legislature. They shot and killed the nation's prime minister and seven members of parliament. Disturbed by the political instability, even more Armenians left their nation—mostly moving to Russia.

A New Century

The assassinations struck a blow to the fragile young republic. But Armenia recovered. Its president, Robert Kocharian, stabilized the government. In 2003 Kocharian again won the presidency—although some people accused his supporters of rigging the vote. The nation's economy continued to improve. The cease-fire with Azerbaijan held, although violence erupted on occasion. New industries, including tourism, began to grow in Armenia.

Armenia continued to reach out to the international community. It joined the World Trade Organization in 2003. When the United States went to war in Iraq in 2003, Armenia contributed a small number of troops to help the Americans and their allies. In 2006 the United States pledged to provide $235 million in aid to Armenia to help reduce poverty, improve roads, and upgrade irrigation networks.

In February 2008, Armenians went to the polls to vote on a new president. The winner was Serhz Sarksyan, who had previously served as prime minister. Opponents charged that Sarksyan's supporters had rigged the ballot. Protestors rioted in Yerevan, and soldiers moved in to impose order, beating and arresting some demonstrators. Western observers said the election was mostly fair, but critics disagree. Clearly, democracy in Armenia is not yet on entirely firm footing.

▷ Government

Armenia is a republic—a nation in which citizens elect their own leaders. All citizens age eighteen and older are eligible to vote.

The president is the head of state. Voters elect the president to a five-year term, with a two-term limit. The president appoints a prime minister to oversee the day-to-day running of the government. The prime minister appoints a group of advisers called the Council of Ministers. The ministers head government departments such as the Ministry of Foreign Affairs and the Ministry of Energy.

Armenia's parliament, or law-making body, is called the National Assembly. It has 131 members. Voters elect 41 of these members directly. That is, people vote for individuals, and the top vote-getters are seated in the legislature. The other 90 members of the National Assembly are elected by party list. In other words, people vote for a

ROOM FOR IMPROVEMENT

Critics have pointed out flaws with the Armenian government. International groups say that Armenia has a poor human rights record. They charge that police sometimes arrest people for no cause, beat prisoners, and hold them in jail without trial. They also say the Armenian government tries to suppress press freedom and political dissent.

Many critics charge that the Armenian government is corrupt. They say high-ranking officials take bribes, break the law, and use their positions to benefit themselves and their business associates. In theory, Armenia is a democracy—which means that power rests in the hands of the people. But critics claim that power in Armenia is really concentrated in the hands of a small group of political and business leaders.

Yerevan's Republic Square features elaborate fountains. Behind the fountains, Government House contains the offices of the Council of Ministers. Traditional Armenian rugs inspired the patterns of the square's pavement.

political party instead of individuals. If a certain party wins 50 percent of the vote, for instance, it wins 50 percent of the 90 party-list seats in the parliament. Members of the National Assembly serve four-year terms.

Armenia has local, regional, and national courts to hear both criminal and civil cases. For matters of local government, the nation is divided into eleven provinces, plus the city of Yerevan. The president appoints governors to run each province. Elected and appointed leaders administer local governments.

> Visit www.vgsbooks.com for links to websites with additional information about the history and government of Armenia. Find out the names of Armenian leaders and read about recent elections.

THE PEOPLE

Armenia is home to about 3 million people. Because of poverty, the nation's birthrate is low. Many married couples can't afford to raise many children. The typical Armenian woman will have one or two children during her lifetime. Since independence, many Armenians have left their nation to escape poverty and violence. This emigration, combined with the low birthrate, has resulted in low population growth. The population is expected to reach only 3.4 million by the year 2025.

◯ Ethnic Groups

Ethnic Armenians make up 98 percent of the population. An ethnic group called Kurds (concentrated in western Armenia) accounts for 1.3 percent. Russians make up 0.5 percent. The remaining 0.2 percent of Armenia's people belong to other ethnic groups. At the time of independence, Armenia had a small (about 3 percent) Azeri population. But during the Nagorno-Karabakh conflict, almost all the Azeris fled Armenia for Azerbaijan.

▶ Urban and Rural Life

The population density in Armenia is 258 people per square mile (100 people per square km). The cities are more densely populated than the countryside. About 64 percent of Armenians live in cities, with one-third of the nation's population in Yerevan. Since independence, many young people have left the countryside for jobs and schooling in Yerevan and other big cities.

Armenia's city dwellers live much like urban people in other parts of the industrially developed world. They work at various jobs, in factories, shops, government offices, banks, and other businesses. They live in small homes or apartment houses—many of them built during the Soviet era. The streets of Armenia's big cities are crowded with cars, taxis, buses, and pedestrians. Some young urban dwellers wear fashionable clothing—similar to styles worn in Europe and the United States. They like to hang out at nightclubs and Internet cafés.

Members of an Armenian Kurdish family relax in their home. The Kurds are known for creating beautiful woven carpets with unique designs.

Rural life is much slower paced. Rural Armenians tend not to follow the latest urban trends and fashions. In fact, many are elderly people, whose younger family members have left for jobs in the city. The Armenian countryside is dotted with small farming villages. People there raise fruits, vegetables, and livestock. Many rural Armenians are subsistence farmers. That is, they are able to raise only enough food to feed themselves, with little or none left over to sell. Other rural Armenians run shops or other small businesses. Some rural towns are very isolated. They are high in the mountains and difficult to reach.

In both cities and rural areas, housing tends to be substandard. Many homes and apartments are crowded and run-down. They lack efficient heating systems and up-to-date plumbing. Some people in Gyumri still live in metal shipping containers that were supposed to serve as only temporary shelters after the 1988 earthquake. These structures are freezing cold in winter and broiling hot in summer.

They lack all amenities such as bathrooms and cooking facilities. Most of Armenia's buildings are not designed to withstand earthquakes. Should another big quake hit an urban area, homes and buildings would once again be destroyed.

Health Care

Health care in Armenia is uneven. Yerevan and other big cities have hospitals, clinics, and well-trained doctors. But many rural areas have poor or no medical facilities. The Armenian government has not invested much in the nation's health care system. Hospitals and clinics have to charge high fees to cover their costs. Even where health care is available, many poor Armenians can't afford it.

Poverty and poor health care have taken their toll on Armenian children. The infant mortality rate (numbers of children who die in infancy) is 21 deaths per 1,000 births—much higher than rates in Western nations. The maternal mortality rate (number of mothers who die from childbirth-related causes) is 19 deaths per 100,000 births—also higher than Western rates. Many poor children do not receive all the vaccines needed to protect them from childhood diseases. Some Armenian children even suffer from malnutrition.

As adults, Armenians tend to suffer from diseases common in other industrialized nations, such as cancer. Many Armenians smoke cigarettes, a habit that leads to cancer, heart disease, stroke, and other health problems. Rates of HIV (human immunodeficiency virus—the virus that causes AIDS) infection are low in Armenia. Only about 0.1 percent of Armenian adults are infected with the virus.

Red Cross nurses examine a child at a free health fair in Yerevan. Many parents cannot afford regular doctor visits for their children.

OLD-TIMERS

Armenia is famous for its long-lived residents. In northern and western Armenia, you can see gravestones of people whose lives spanned more than one hundred years. People in other parts of the Caucasus are also famously long lived.

Doctors aren't sure why some people in this area live so long. It could be the brisk mountain air or the clean mountain water. Or maybe some people have longevity in their genes. But the truth is that despite the occasional centenarian (person older than one hundred), most people in Armenia do not live longer than people in other places. Men typically die in their sixties and women in their seventies.

An elderly Armenian man sits outside his home in a remote village. He wears a style of clothing that has not changed in more than a hundred years.

Life expectancy in Armenia is about 69 years for men and 76 years for women. These figures are lower than those of Western nations but much higher than rates in the world's poorest countries.

Education

Armenia has a history of literacy—dating back to the creation of the Armenian alphabet in the early 400s. The nation has long valued education. During the Soviet era, Armenian schools were top level. Since independence, Armenia has struggled to keep providing high-quality education to its young people. The government does not have a big budget for education. Some schools are poorly equipped. Teachers are not well paid. Nevertheless, Armenia remains a well-educated nation. Its literacy rate (percentage of people who can read and write) is 99 percent.

Children share desks at a public elementary school in an Armenian town. Boys and girls sit on opposite sides of the room.

Some parents send their children to private, church-run schools. Other Armenians attend public schools. Public schooling is free for all children ages six through sixteen. The curriculum includes the Armenian language, literature, and history. Students also learn math, science, geography, and other academic subjects. Although some students drop out before completing their education, enrollment rates are high.

Armenia has more than forty schools for higher education. These institutions include colleges, universities, and vocational

Under Soviet rule, Armenian children studied the Russian language as well as their native Armenian. But Armenians preferred their own language to Russian. With the end of Soviet rule, Armenia dropped Russian from its school curriculum. Some Armenians still speak Russian as a second language, but their numbers are dwindling as a new generation grows up without Russian-language education.

Yerevan State University takes pride in educating students in Armenian history and literature, as well as in computer programming, science, and other fields.

(job-training) schools. More than 70,000 Armenians are enrolled in some form of higher education. The nation's largest university is Yerevan State University. It has about 10,000 students.

Visit www.vgsbooks.com for links to websites with additional information about education in Armenia. Read about the Armenian school system and get the latest news about Yerevan State University.

Women's Roles

In earlier centuries, Armenia was a patriarchal society. That is, the father was the head of the household. His wife and children were expected to obey him. Women were supposed to care for their homes and children and did not take part in business or government. Few girls attended school.

An **Armenian mother** holds her son at the rocky edge of a soccer field.

This age-old situation changed during the Soviet era. Under the Soviet system, women were treated equally with men. Boys and girls received the same education. Many women held high-level jobs in business and government. The Soviet government ran child-care centers so that women were free to hold full-time jobs.

With the breakup of the Soviet Union, Armenia has returned to some of its old patriarchal attitudes. According to the nation's constitution, women and men have equal rights. Males and females attend school in equal numbers in Armenia. But women often suffer discrimination in the workplace. Many employers refuse to hire or promote women. Women hold only 5 percent of seats in Armenia's parliament.

Some of the worst treatment of women occurs in the home. Women's rights groups report high rates of domestic violence in Armenia. Men beat and sometimes even kill their wives. Police often ignore domestic violence complaints, and abusive husbands go unpunished.

CULTURAL LIFE

Armenia is an ancient nation. Its religion and literature date to the early centuries A.D. Its artistic and musical roots are even older. Armenia sits at the crossroads between Europe, Asia, and the Middle East. The Greeks, Romans, Persians, Russians, Ottomans, and other groups ruled the nation at different times in the past. Armenian culture reflects the influences of these different rulers. The culture has changed with the times. In the twentieth century, the Soviet Union had a big influence on Armenian culture. In the twenty-first century, Armenians enjoy films, music, and other cultural offerings from the West. Yet they remain intimately connected to their ancient cultural heritage.

 ## Religion

Christianity is the dominant religion in Armenia. In the early fourth century A.D., Armenia was the first nation to adopt Christianity as its official religion. In the early years, the Armenian Apostolic Church was affiliated with the main Christian church based in Rome. But

in 451, after a disagreement over the nature of Jesus, the Armenian Church and several others broke from the Roman church. As a result, the Armenian Apostolic Church practices different rites than Christian churches in much of the rest of the world.

During the Stalinist era, the Soviet government tried to suppress all religion. It shut down Armenian churches and killed some church leaders. Later in the twentieth century, the Soviet government relaxed restrictions on religious worship. Churches reopened, and Armenians again worshipped freely. In modern Armenia, freedom of religion is guaranteed under the nation's constitution.

About 95 percent of Armenians belong to the Armenian Apostolic Church, while about 4 percent belong to other Christian denominations. About 1 percent of Armenians—members of the nation's small Kurdish community—practice Yezidism. This religion combines elements of Islamic, Zoroastrian, Jewish, and pre-Christian beliefs. Yezidism dates to the seventh century A.D.

In earlier centuries, small numbers of Azeris lived in Armenia. Most of them practiced Islam. During the war over Nagorno-Karabakh, almost all the Azeris fled Armenia for Azerbaijan. With the Azeri population drastically reduced, Islam has almost disappeared in Armenia. In the twenty-first century, Muslim Armenians make up only a tiny fraction of the nation's population. Most of them are Kurds.

Language and Literature

Armenian is one of the world's oldest living languages. People have been speaking Armenian since the 600s B.C., perhaps even earlier. Armenian belongs to the large Indo-European family of languages. This language family includes most of the languages spoken in modern-day Europe, the Americas, Russia and the former Soviet republics, and Iran.

Over the centuries, Armenia has borrowed words from the languages of its neighbors and conquerors. Many Armenian words come from Turkish and from Farsi—the language of Iran. The Armenian language has also split into different dialects, or variations. Grabar is an old dialect from the early centuries A.D. In modern times, it is used only for church services. For day-to-day communication, people in Armenia use a dialect called Eastern Armenian. Western Armenian is a dialect from Turkey. Many members of the diaspora speak this dialect. People who speak Western and Eastern Armenian can usually understand each other, even though some of the words and grammar are different.

The cleric Mesrob created the Armenian alphabet in the fifth century A.D. The new alphabet ushered in a period of literacy in Armenia. Scholars began to translate religious writings and other texts into Armenian. They also wrote original works. In the fifth, sixth, and seventh centuries, several scholars wrote histories of Armenia. These

LANGUAGE LESSON

Here are a few common words and phrases and their Armenian translations. Since the Armenian alphabet looks entirely different than the Roman alphabet (used for English and the common languages of Europe), the Armenian words have been transliterated. That is, they are spelled out using Roman instead of Armenian letters.

ENGLISH	ARMENIAN
Hello	Barev
Good-bye	Tstesootyoon
Please	Khndroom em
Thank you	Shnorhakalatyoon
Yes	Ayo
No	Votch
Good	Lav
Bad	Vat
What's your name?	Anunut eench eh?

Mesrob based the **Armenian alphabet** on the curved forms of Greek letters.

texts tell the stories of kings, church leaders, wars, and other historic events.

In the tenth century, Armenian writers branched out into poetry. Poets wrote about religion, history, and love. Some of the works were epics, or extremely long poems. One epic, *David of Sassoun*, describes Armenia's struggles against Muslim rulers in the seventh and eighth centuries.

In the 1800s, Armenians began writing novels. These books explored life in Armenian villages, struggles against foreign occupiers, and other timely topics. In the early twentieth century, writers became more and more political. They wrote about Armenian nationalism (the desire for a self-governing Armenia), the Armenian genocide, and life under Soviet rule. Armenian writers had to be extremely careful during the Soviet era, however. The Soviet government did not allow free speech. Writers who criticized the government could be arrested. To

A statue in Republic Square in Yerevan celebrates **David of Sassoun,** the hero of an epic poem from tenth-century Armenia.

publish their works freely, many writers escaped to the West during the mid-twentieth century.

One of the most famous Armenian writers was not born in Armenia. He was William Saroyan, the son of Armenian immigrants to the United States. Saroyan was an acclaimed novelist and playwright. After his death in 1981, his body was cremated. Half of the ashes were buried in the Pantheon of Greats, a graveyard for famous Armenians in Yerevan.

An Ancient Craft

Armenia is famous for its colorful, brilliantly designed woolen rugs. Examples date back to the 700s B.C. Early Armenian rugs were used not only as floor coverings but also as window curtains, blankets, and furniture coverings. Ancient craftspeople developed elaborate designs and patterns. They used vegetable dyes to impart brilliant colors to the wool. By the Middle Ages (about A.D. 500 to 1500), Armenian rugs had become famous. Traders carried them to Europe and Asia. By the nineteenth century, rug making was a big business in Armenia as well as in diaspora communities. Workshops employed hundreds of weavers. During the Soviet era, some factories produced machine-made rugs. But a few people continued to weave rugs by hand at home. Since independence, the Armenian rug industry has undergone a revival. People restore antique rugs, study the old designs, and produce new rugs by hand using traditional tools and techniques.

Folk Art and Fine Art

The Armenian artistic tradition dates to prehistoric times. Petroglyphs—pictures carved on rocks—show deer, boars, wolves, foxes, snakes, and other wild animals. Some pictures depict domesticated animals (animals adapted to life with people), such as dogs and goats. Others show hunters carrying bows, clubs, and other weapons. Still other carvings are pictures of the Sun, the Moon, the stars, and lightning.

Later, after they settled down and became farmers, Armenians worked with metal. They used bronze, gold, and other metals to create knives, armor, and other useful objects. They also created gold and silver jewelry, clay pottery, wooden furniture, and woolen carpets. These objects were not only useful but also beautiful. Armenian craftspeople continued to fashion objects out of metal, clay, wood, and fabrics into the modern era.

After Armenia became a Christian nation, artists began to make religious artworks. They created illuminated manuscripts. These religious

This **illuminated page** comes from a religious manuscript that was created in about A.D. 989.

texts were decorated with lush illustrations. The pictures surrounding the texts showed the apostles (Jesus's early followers) and other religious scenes. The books were often bound with decorative ivory or metal covers. Most Armenian illuminated manuscripts date from the ninth to the seventeenth centuries.

In the nineteenth century, influenced by Russian and European artists, many Armenians worked as painters. They created portraits, landscapes, religious images, and scenes of daily life. One Armenian painter—Arshile Gorky—achieved international acclaim. Gorky was born in Turkish-held Armenia but immigrated to the United States as a teenager. He became a leading member of the abstract expressionism movement, a group of artists who created nontraditional and nonrepresentational works.

Architecture

Armenia's architecture is one of its greatest national treasures. Early builders used basalt, tuff, limestone, and other native rocks to create magnificent structures throughout historic Armenia. Only a few buildings remain from Armenia's pre-Christian era. One of them is a Greco (Greek)-Roman-style temple at the city of Garni. It dates to either the first or second century A.D.

With the arrival of Christianity, Armenians began to build churches. Many of them were built on the foundations of pre-Christian shrines. The most common building material was tuff, a stone that is strong but easily carved. Many churches were built according to a standardized plan, with the building shaped as either a square or a cross. Inside,

When leaving an Armenian church, it is proper to walk backward, so as not to turn your back on God.

many churches had beautiful frescoes (wall paintings) and elaborate stone carvings.

Monasteries are communities of people who have devoted their lives to God. Armenia is famous for its monasteries. Many of them date to the tenth century or earlier. The most famous Armenian monasteries command breathtaking sites, perched on cliffs or inside rocky gorges. Monastery buildings typically include churches and chapels, mausoleums (burial chambers), libraries, residences, and work buildings. Monasteries are popular destinations for modern-day tourists and pilgrims (religious travelers) in Armenia. Other interesting buildings are centuries-old fortresses and inns for travelers called caravanserais.

CROSS STONES

Tall, flat stones called *khachkars* are a common sight in Armenia. The word *khachkar* means "cross stone" in Armenian. Most stones are carved with crosses (representing Jesus), surrounded by ornate floral or geometric designs. The khachkars are memorial stones. They are sometimes placed above graves like tombstones. Others commemorate military victories or the building of a church or another important structure. Still others are erected to protect people against bad fortune. Armenia's monasteries have many khachkars. Some of them are embedded in church walls and others stand outside. Armenians have been creating khachkars since at least the ninth century. Modern-day Armenians still erect khachkars to honor people and events.

An elaborate khachkar stands above a grave in Noratus. The village cemetery is famous for its collection of khachkars, some dating to medieval times.

When the Soviet Union took over Armenia, it introduced a new building style to the nation. In Yerevan, Soviet architects erected massive stone buildings, fountains, plazas, and statues. The structures were meant to reflect the heroism and greatness of the Soviet Union. In the twenty-first century, Armenian towns and cities reflect a mix of architectural styles, with everything from old stone houses to Soviet-era apartment buildings to modern skyscrapers.

Music and Dance

In earlier centuries, Armenians sang folksongs about love, work, history, and daily life. Musicians played homemade instruments. They fashioned stringed instruments out of wood and strings of animal gut. They made drums from wood and animal skins. They built wind instruments from wood and reeds. People made music with friends at home and on special occasions, such as weddings. In modern times, many revival bands perform folk music with traditional instruments. The high-pitched sound of the reed instruments is prominent in Armenian folk music.

An instrument maker repairs a *tar*, a lutelike Armenian instrument. On the table, a stringed *kemenche* leans against a *dhol*, which is a double-sided drum.

Dancing is also part of the Armenian folk tradition. In earlier eras, people danced at parties and festivals. Some dances were for men only; others for women only. Line dances were common. In modern Armenia and many parts of the diaspora, dance troupes perform the old dances. Dancers wear traditional costumes—brightly colored dresses and veiled hats for women, trousers and embroidered tunics for men. Ordinary Armenians also still dance at weddings, parties, and other special occasions.

Liturgical music—performed during Christian worship—is another Armenian tradition. Singers perform unaccompanied by instruments. The melodies are hauntingly beautiful. Some of the songs are more than one thousand years old.

In the nineteenth century, the Russians introduced Western classical music and ballet to Armenia. Armenians quickly embraced classical

Folk dancers perform a traditional dance in the village of Garni.

Musaha is an Armenian dish made with eggplant and peppers. *Lavash* (flatbread) sits to the right of the main dish.

music. In the twentieth century, musicians in Yerevan established orchestras, operas, and ballet troupes. The classical music tradition remains strong throughout Armenia. Armenians also enjoy rock, pop, jazz, and other modern musical styles.

Food

Armenia offers a delicious cuisine, highlighted by spicy meats, fresh salads, and chewy flatbread. The recipes date back many centuries. Over the years, Armenian chefs borrowed recipes and ingredients from Persian, Arabic, Turkish, Russian, Greek, and other neighboring cuisines.

Barbecue is a staple of the Armenian diet. Pork is the most commonly barbecued meat, although cooks also barbecue lamb, beef, chicken, and fish. Spicy sausages are popular, as is smoked fish. Lamb stew comes in many variations, with ingredients such as apricots, artichokes, and leeks added to enhance the flavor. Meat dishes are usually served with rice or bulgur (cracked wheat).

Armenians love salads. Cucumber and tomato salad, green bean salad, and potato salad are just a few of the dozens of variations made with vegetables, herbs, beans, peas, fruits, nuts, eggs, and meat. Cold, summer soups are made with yogurt, cucumber, and fruit. Hot lamb soup is a hearty winter dish. Dolmas—grape or cabbage leaves stuffed with rice and meat—make a tasty side dish. Cheese and spinach pastries are other favorites. Armenians eat a flatbread called *lavash* at almost every meal.

Armenians usually eat fresh fruit and cheese for dessert. They also like pastries, such as baklava. This treat is made with layers of paperlike filo dough stuffed with nuts, fruit, and cheese and then covered with honey, sugar, or syrup. People also eat dried apricots, peaches, and plums for a snack or dessert. Nuts are another well-loved snack.

ARMENIAN BEAN SALAD

Armenians make an endless variety of salads using vegetables, beans, fruits, and other ingredients. This bean salad is tasty and easy to make.

1 (20-ounce) can large white kidney beans

1 medium to large onion

1 cup fresh parsley, finely chopped

1 tomato, cut into wedges

lemon juice

salt and pepper

1 green bell pepper, sliced into rings

salad dressing, such as Italian or oil and vinegar

1. Drain liquid from can of beans and rinse beans.
2. Cut onion into slivers. Sprinkle with salt and let stand for 30 minutes.
3. Rinse onion, and pat it dry with paper towel.
4. Combine beans, onion, and parsley. Put salad into refrigerator to chill.
5. Before serving, add tomato wedges, squirt with lemon juice, season with salt and pepper, and garnish with pepper rings.
6. Serve with salad dressing.

Serves 4 to 5

Armenians like strong black coffee, sweetened with a little sugar. Tea is another popular drink. Armenia is world famous for its brandy, an alcoholic drink made from wine or fruit juice. The water from Armenia's mountain springs is clean, clear, and delicious. People can drink the water straight from the spring, without worrying about getting sick.

Holidays and Festivals

Armenians celebrate both religious and nonreligious holidays. They observe Christmas on January 6—the day of the baptism of Jesus, according to Armenian church teaching. They observe Easter in March or April, depending on the church calendar.

Some Armenian holidays have their roots in folk beliefs. For instance, forty days after Christmas, Armenians celebrate a holiday called Trndez, or Purification. On this day, people light bonfires and leap over them for protection from evil spirits. Trndez also marks the coming of spring. A holiday called Saint Sargis Day takes place nine weeks before Easter. On this holiday, a young woman may dream of a

An Armenian priest blesses hundreds of red-dyed eggs. The eggs are part of the traditional Armenian celebration of Easter.

handsome warrior wearing gold armor. According to folk belief, this man will be her husband.

Vardevar is a religious holiday with its roots in ancient tradition. In pre-Christian Armenia, Vardevar honored a love goddess. People observed the holiday by showering each other with rose petals. In modern times, Vardevar commemorates an event from the New Testament (the Christian books of the Bible), when Jesus climbed up Mount Sinai to talk with the prophets Moses and Elijah. Modern Armenians (especially children) celebrate the holiday by throwing buckets of water on their friends and neighbors. They throw water off balconies and into open car windows. Vardevar falls on a different day each summer, depending on the church calendar.

In pre-Christian times, Armenians celebrated the New Year on the first day of August. In modern times, New Year's Day is January 1. On this day, each family bakes cookies and a loaf of New Year bread. The loaf contains a coin. Whoever finds the coin is supposed to get good luck in the coming year.

Some Armenian holidays commemorate important historic events. For instance, Independence Day, September 21, marks Armenia's official break with the Soviet Union in 1991. Earthquake Memorial

On May 28, 2005, **more than 150,000 Armenians formed a human chain** around Mount Aragats and performed a traditional dance. They were celebrating the birthday of the first Armenian republic.

Day, December 7, recalls the disastrous 1988 earthquake. On April 24, Armenians observe Genocide Memorial Day to honor the victims of the World War I genocide. On May 9 they remember the Allied victory in World War II. On May 28 they recall their short-lived first republic. Other holidays honor the nation's army (January 28), mothers (April 7), and the constitution (July 5).

Visit www.vgsbooks.com for links to websites with additional information about Armenia's holiday celebrations. Listen to samples of Armenian music and play videos of traditional dances.

Sports and Recreation

A small nation, Armenia does not have world-class sports facilities or teams. However, many Armenians excel in fighting sports, such as wrestling, boxing, and judo. Others show their talent in soccer, ice hockey, basketball, and weightlifting. Several members of the diaspora have become world-champion athletes. The most famous is Andre Agassi, an Armenian American tennis player.

During the Soviet era, Armenian athletes won Olympic medals on behalf of the Soviet Union. Since 1994 Armenia has participated in the Olympics as an independent nation. At the 1996 Summer Games in the U.S. city of Atlanta, Georgia, Armenian wrestler Armen Nazaryan won a gold medal in Greco-Roman wrestling in the flyweight category—becoming independent Armenia's first Olympic gold medalist.

Chess is extremely popular among young Armenians. The country has produced many chess champions, and Armenia's national team is a strong force in international tournaments. Russian politician Gary Kasparov is the most famous of all Armenian chess champions. Older Armenians tend to prefer a board game called backgammon to chess.

Armenia is a wonderful place for outdoor adventure. The town of Tsaghkadzor has a world-class ski resort. Lake Sevan offers sailing and windsurfing. Many travelers come to Armenia to hike in the mountains and nature reserves. Some people climb Mount Aragats. Many outdoor sports require high-tech, high-priced gear, which most ordinary Armenians can't afford. As a result, most people who partake in adventure sports in Armenia are foreign tourists.

Workers at a Yerevan electronics company play backgammon during a break. The game of backgammon may be more than five thousand years old.

THE ECONOMY

Armenia's economy, after plummeting immediately after independence, has been steadily growing. The gross domestic product (GDP)—the measure of all goods and services produced in the nation in one year—was $5 billion dollars in 2005. Between 2005 and 2008, GDP grew by more than 10 percent each year. Inflation rates (rate of rising prices) are fairly low. Many foreign companies have opened businesses in Armenia.

However, the economy still has trouble spots. About 7.4 percent of Armenia's workforce is unemployed. An estimated 26 percent of Armenians live below the poverty line. Armenia also has trouble obtaining all the products it needs from outside nations. Since the war over Nagorno-Karabakh, both Azerbaijan and Turkey have refused to trade with Armenia. They have closed their borders with Armenia—preventing the flow of goods and fuel back and forth. Armenia trades with its neighbors Iran, Georgia, and Russia, as well as more distant nations, but the hostilities with Azerbaijan and Turkey have caused lasting economic difficulties.

○ Agriculture

The agricultural sector includes farming, fishing, and forestry. Agriculture accounts for about 17 percent of Armenia's GDP. About 45 percent of workers are employed in agriculture. Farming makes up the biggest portion of the Armenian agricultural sector. The nation's timber and fishing industries are fairly small.

About 20 percent of the nation's land is suitable for growing crops. Because of low rainfall, farmers must use irrigation systems to bring water to their fields. Chief agricultural areas are the Araks River valley and Ararat Plain.

Farmers grow a variety of fruits and vegetables (including grapes, cherries, apricots, figs, olives, and tomatoes), roots (including potatoes, yams, and beets), and nuts and seeds (including almonds, pistachios, and sunflower seeds). They grow grains such as wheat, corn, and barley. In mountainous areas, farmers raise livestock such as sheep, goats, and cattle. The animals yield meat, milk, wool, and skins.

Many Armenians are subsistence farmers, growing just enough food to feed their families. Other farmers run large-scale operations. They sell products both nationally and internationally. The main agricultural exports (products sold to other nations) are brandy, fruit juices, animal skins, and tomatoes.

◉ Industry

The industrial sector includes manufacturing, mining, and energy production. Industry accounts for about 36 percent of GDP and employs about 25 percent of the nation's workforce.

Armenia had a strong manufacturing sector during the Soviet era. After independence, the sector went into decline. Equipment had become old and outdated. Manufacturers struggled for several years to upgrade their operations.

In the 2000s, manufacturing has been revived in Armenia. Some factories produce machine tools, electric motors, tires, shoes, clothing, chemicals, trucks, fertilizers, building materials, and other products. Other factories process agricultural products—turning fruit into wine and brandy, for instance, or sunflower seeds into oil. New and growing

This factory, located in Yerevan, makes rubber and latex products. It was founded in the 1940s.

In 2007 former Armenian president Robert Kocharian *(right)* joined President Mahmoud Ahmadinejad *(left)* of Iran at a ceremony opening a **new pipeline for natural gas** at the Armenia-Iran border.

areas of Armenia's manufacturing sector include diamond processing (the diamonds do not come from Armenia, however), jewelry making, and microelectronics.

Armenia has a small mining industry, with reserves of copper, molybdenum, zinc, gold, silver, lead, granite, and marble. Armenia uses these minerals in its own building and manufacturing operations. It also exports some minerals to foreign nations.

Experts believe that Armenia has small amounts of coal, oil, and natural gas. But the rugged mountain terrain makes it extremely difficult and expensive to extract these resources, so they remain undeveloped. Armenia generates electricity at several hydroelectric plants. The Metsamor nuclear plant provides a large portion of the nation's power. Finally, Armenia imports oil and natural gas from Russia and other countries. It also built a pipeline to bring in natural gas from Iran.

The Armenian government plans to shut down the dangerous Metsamor nuclear power plant as soon as it can secure alternative sources of energy.

Services

The service sector includes banking, insurance, government, sales, communications, education, and other businesses that provide services instead of making products. Service businesses account for 47 percent of Armenia's GDP. About 30 percent of Armenian workers are employed in the service sector.

Tourism is a growing service business in Armenia. The nation has breathtaking mountain scenery and fascinating historic buildings. Yerevan is a cultural magnet with dozens of museums, historic sites, and musical venues. Armenia's monasteries are particularly compelling for Christian visitors. The government actively promotes the nation as a tourist destination. In the early 2000s, more than 120,000 foreign tourists visited Armenia each year. These visitors added more than $65 million to the nation's economy each year.

Visit www.vgsbooks.com for links to websites with additional information about tourism in Armenia. Find out what you need to plan a visit and get a glimpse of Armenia's biggest attractions.

Transportation

Being a landlocked nation has hurt Armenia economically. It has no seaports for shipping or receiving cargo. Although it has several rivers, they are not large enough for boat traffic. Goods have to travel to and from Armenia either by air (on cargo planes) or overland (on trucks and trains). Since the early 1990s, both Azerbaijan and Turkey have closed their land borders with Armenia. This blockade has restricted trade even further.

Armenia has ten airports with paved runways and two unpaved airfields. The main airport is the Zvartnots Airport in Yerevan. It offers service to cities in Turkey, the Middle East, Europe, Russia, and the other former Soviet republics.

People traveling within Armenia can take trains, buses, shuttle buses, or cars. Armenia has 4,742 miles (7,633 km) of paved roads, but many of them are in poor repair. Driving on the steep mountain roads can be harrowing. The streets of Yerevan are crowded with private cars, taxis, buses, and shuttle buses.

THE DARK SIDE

The Armenian economy has a sinister side. Drug traffickers operate in Armenia. They use the nation as a transit point for shipments of opium and hashish traveling from Asia to Russia and Europe. Armenia also has a problem with human trafficking. Traffickers sometimes seize poor Armenian women and girls and force them to work as prostitutes in Turkey, the Middle East, and other places. The Armenian government tries to fight drug and human trafficking, but the problems persist.

Communications

At independence, Armenia's telecommunications network was outdated. Since then, the nation has been upgrading and expanding its systems. Private companies have run fiber-optic cables and set up satellite networks to provide reliable national and international phone service. In 2005 Armenia had about 600,000 landlines and 318,000 cell phone users. In 2006 it had 173,000 Internet users. These numbers continue to grow as communication systems improve.

Armenia has four private and two public television stations. Viewers can also tune in shows from Russia. Those with satellite TV can get programs from Europe and the United States. Twenty-five radio stations offer a variety of programming—from sports to news to music. Armenian newsstands overflow with daily and weekly newspapers. Major dailies include *Aravot*, *AZG*, and *Yerkir*.

In theory, Armenians enjoy freedom of the press and freedom of speech. But the reality is different. The Armenian government has harassed and tried to shut down news outlets that have criticized national leaders. To play it safe, many Armenian journalists censor themselves. That is, they choose not to report news stories or express opinions that might get them in trouble with the government.

The Future

In 2011 Armenia will celebrate its twentieth anniversary as an independent nation. It seems to be on the road to prosperity. Its economy operates in high gear. If growth continues, the nation should see higher rates of employment and less poverty. After a troubled start, Armenia's political systems have stabilized. International observers say that the 2008 presidential elections were fair, although some citizens cried foul.

The international community is working with Armenia to improve its human rights record and to strengthen its democratic practices. The international community also helps Armenia with large amounts of financial aid. Additional money, as well as moral support, constantly pours in from the far-flung Armenian diaspora. Many people have a keen interest in seeing this small democracy succeed and flourish.

Of course, the nation faces obstacles. Another earthquake could severely damage buildings and roads and other structures. Hostilities with Azerbaijan have not died down completely. Economic blockades still hurt Armenia's foreign trade. Energy supplies are precarious. Nevertheless, Armenia's success seems certain. It has a highly educated population. It has a long history of business achievement, national pride, and artistic excellence. The dark days of foreign occupation are over. In all likelihood, Armenia will have a bright future.

ca. 10,000 B.C.	People settle into farming villages in territory that later becomes Armenia.
1300s B.C.	Tribes join together to create the kingdom of Urartu, centered at Lake Van.
600s B.C.	The ancestors of present-day Armenians move to Urartu.
500s B.C.	Urartu falls to the Medes and then the Persians.
331 B.C.	Alexander the Great conquers Persia, thereby bringing Armenia into the Greek Empire.
95 B.C.	Tigranes the Great conquers surrounding territory and creates an Armenian Empire.
36 B.C.	Tigranes's son Artavasdes surrenders his empire to the Roman Empire.
A.D. 301 or 314	King Tiridates III makes Christianity the official religion of Armenia.
early 400s	Mesrob creates the Armenian alphabet. The Byzantines and the Persians divide Armenia between them.
451	Armenians fight the Persians at the Battle of Avarayr. The Armenian Apostolic Church splits with the main Christian church in Rome.
640	An Islamic army from the Arabian Peninsula conquers Armenia.
885	Ashot I becomes king of Armenia, ushering in a period of artistic and literary growth.
1071	The Seljuk Turks defeat the Armenians at the Battle of Manzikert.
1080	Armenians create a kingdom in Cilicia.
1639	The Ottoman Turks take over western Armenia. The Persians take eastern Armenia.
1700s	The Russian Empire takes over eastern Armenia.
1894–1896	Turkish authorities massacre 300,000 Armenians.
1914	World War I breaks out in Europe.
1915	The Turks begin to systematically massacre Armenians. By 1918 they have killed about 1.5 million Armenians.
1918	Armenians create an independent republic.
1920	Armenia surrenders to Russian communists. Yerevan State University is founded.

1922   Armenia, Georgia, and Azerbaijan are combined into the Transcaucasian Soviet Federated Republic, part of the new Soviet Union.

mid-1920s   Architects rebuild Yerevan according to a Soviet master plan.

1934   Soviet leader Joseph Stalin begins purges in the Soviet Union. He kills at least 100,000 Armenians. He also attacks the Armenian Apostolic Church. The purges will last until 1939.

1936   Armenia becomes the separate Armenian Soviet Socialist Republic.

1939-1945   World nations fight World War II. About 630,000 Armenians serve in the Soviet military.

1965   Thousands of Armenian demonstrators march through the streets of Yerevan to commemorate the fiftieth anniversary of the Armenian Genocide. The Soviet government calls in troops to quiet protests.

1985   Soviet leader Mikhail Gorbachev introduces *glasnost* and *perestroika* to the Soviet Union. Armenians welcome the new openness and begin to talk about Armenian independence.

1988   Armenia and Azerbaijan begin fighting over control of Nagorno-Karabakh. A major earthquake strikes northwestern Armenia in December.

1990   The Armenian Pannational Movement takes control in Armenia.

1991   Armenians vote for independence from the Soviet Union. They elect Levon Ter-Petrossian as their first president.

1994   Armenia and Azerbaijan declare a cease-fire in the Nagorno-Karabakh conflict.

1995   Armenian voters approve a new constitution.

1996   Wrestler Armen Nazaryan wins the first Olympic gold medal for independent Armenia.

1999   Assassins kill Armenia's prime minister and seven members of parliament.

2003   Armenia joins the World Trade Organization. Armenia sends a small number of soldiers to assist the U.S.-led invasion of Iraq.

2008   Armenians elect Serhz Sarksyan as their new president. Protestors riot in Yerevan.

Currency Fast Facts

COUNTRY NAME: Republic of Armenia

AREA: 11,506 square miles (29,800 sq. km)

MAIN LANDFORMS: Ararat Plain, Armenian Highland, Bazum Mountains, Dzhavakhet Mountains, Geghama Mountains, Shakhdag Mountains, Vardenis Mountains, Zangezur Mountains

HIGHEST POINT: Mount Aragats, 13,418 feet (4,090 m)

LOWEST POINT: Debed River, 1,320 feet (400 m)

MAJOR RIVERS: Agstev, Araks, Arpa, Debed, Hrazdan

ANIMALS: boars, jackals, lammergeyers, lynxes, mouflon, mountain goats, sheep, Sevan trout, Syrian bears, wildcats

CAPITAL CITY: Yerevan

OTHER MAJOR CITIES: Gyumri, Vagharshapat, Vanadzor

OFFICIAL LANGUAGE: Armenian

MONETARY UNIT: Dram. 1 dram = 100 lumma

CURRENCY

During the Soviet era, Armenia used Soviet money, whose main unit of currency was the ruble. In 1993 Armenia adopted its own currency. The main unit is the dram. The word *dram* means "money" in Armenian. In 2008 it took 307 drams to equal one U.S. dollar.

The Armenian government issues 10-, 20-, 50-, 100-, 200-, and 500-dram coins. It issues 1,000-, 5,000-, 10,000-, 20,000-, and 50,000-dram banknotes (paper money). The banknotes feature pictures of famous Armenians, such as architect Alexander Tamanian and author Yeghishe Charents *(above)*.

Each dram is divided into 100 *lumma*. Originally, the Armenian government issued 10-, 20-, and 50-lumma coins. But people no longer use the coins, since they're worth so little money.

Armenia's flag has three equal horizontal stripes. Red is on top, then blue and then orange. Red symbolizes the blood spilled by Armenian soldiers, blue stands for the Armenian sky, and orange symbolizes Armenia's land. Armenia used the same flag between 1918 and 1920, during the first republic. Armenia readopted the flag when it declared its independence in 1991.

Flag

Armenia's national anthem is "Mer Hayrenik" (Our Fatherland). The words are from a nineteenth-century poem by Miqayel Nalbandyan. Barsegh Kanachyan wrote the melody in the early twentieth century. Armenia used the anthem during the first republic. It readopted the anthem, but with some of the words changed, in 1991. Here are the words translated into English:

National Anthem

Our fatherland, free and independent,
That lived from century to century,
His children are calling,
Free independent Armenia.

Here brother, for you a flag,
That I made with my hands,
Nights I didn't sleep,
With tears I washed it.

Look at it, three colors,
It's our gifted symbol.
Let it shine against the enemy.
Let Armenia always be glorious.

Everywhere death is the same,
Everyone dies only once,
But lucky is the one,
Who is sacrificed for his nation.

> For a link to a site where you can listen to Armenia's national anthem, "Mer Hayrenik," visit www.vgsbooks.com.

LEVON ARONIAN (b. 1982) Aronian is an Armenian chess champion. He was born in Yerevan. He began to play chess at age nine and won the world under-twelve (years old) championship in 1994. He became a grand master, the highest ranking for a chess player, in 2001. In 2002 he became the world junior champion. He followed that victory with numerous wins in adult chess tournaments. In 2008 Aronian was the tenth-highest-rated chess player in the world.

DAVID AZARIAN (1952–2003) Azarian, an acclaimed jazz pianist, was born in Yerevan. He began playing piano at age seven. In the 1960s, he discovered American jazz music by listening to the U.S. Voice of America radio station. In the 1970s, Azarian formed a jazz trio that toured Europe and the Soviet Union. He emigrated to the United States in 1989. Azarian became an assistant professor at the prestigious Berklee College of Music in Boston, Massachusetts. He performed at Carnegie Hall, Birdland, and the Blue Note in New York, as well as other musical venues. He also recorded several CDs. Azarian died in a car crash in Massachusetts in 2003.

ATOM EGOYAN (b. 1960) Filmmaker Atom Egoyan was born to Armenian parents in Cairo, Egypt. Egoyan's family moved to Victoria, British Columbia, Canada, when he was a boy. He attended college at the University of Toronto. Since the late 1970s, he has produced and directed more than fifty films. Several of his works, including *Calendar* (1993) and *Ararat* (2002), examine Armenian history and identity. *Ararat* includes a "film within a film" about the Armenian genocide. Egoyan has earned two Oscar nominations for his work and has won numerous other film awards.

ARSHILE GORKY (1904–1948) Gorky was born in the village of Khorkom in Turkish-held Armenia. His name at birth was Vosdanig Adoian. In 1915, with the start of the Armenian genocide, he and his family fled to Russian-controlled Armenia. In 1920 he moved to the United States and changed his name. Gorky studied painting at the New School of Design in Boston. Afterward, he moved to New York, where he taught art and worked as a painter. Gorky painted images of plants and human figures, but he often distorted them into unusual, abstract shapes. Much of his work falls into the surrealist, cubist, and abstract expressionist categories.

KIRK KERKORIAN (b. 1917) Kerkorian, a U.S. billionaire of Armenian descent, has given hundreds of millions of dollars to assist independent Armenia. Kerkorian was born in Fresno, California. As a young man, he learned to fly airplanes and later bought an airline. Kerkorian then launched a business empire. He bought real estate, hotels, the MGM movie studio, and other businesses. In the process, he became extremely wealthy. In the 1990s, Kerkorian began sending money to Armenia for earthquake relief, housing, social welfare, and other assistance for Armenians. In 2000 he established the Lincy Foundation. This Los Angeles–based charity also funds building and social welfare programs in Armenia.

MAGDALENA MALEEVA (b. 1975) Tennis pro Magdalena Maleeva was born in Sophia, Bulgaria. Her ancestors had fled to Bulgaria after the massacres of Armenians in the Ottoman Empire in the late 1800s. Maleeva's mother was a Bulgarian tennis champion in the 1960s. Her two sisters are also professional tennis players. Maleeva turned pro in 1989. In the 1990s and early 2000s, she won ten Women's Tennis Association tournaments and one International Tennis Federation tournament. She represented Bulgaria at the 1992, 1996, and 2004 Olympic Games. She retired from tennis in 2005.

HASMIK PAPIAN (b. 1961) Papian is a world-renowned opera singer. She was born in Yerevan and studied music at the Yerevan Conservatory. She has performed the world's great operas at venues throughout Europe and the United States. A soprano (the highest singing voice for women), Papian has recorded CDs and won numerous international competitions. She lives in Vienna, Austria.

WILLIAM SAROYAN (1908–1981) Saroyan was born in Fresno, California. His parents were Armenian immigrants to the United States, and the family lived in Fresno's "Armenia Town." After dropping out of high school, Saroyan took up fiction writing. He achieved his first success in 1934 with the publication of a short story collection, *The Daring Young Man on the Flying Trapeze*. In 1943 Saroyan published a novel, *The Human Comedy*, which was made into a movie. He continued to write stories and plays for the rest of his life, garnering international fame and numerous honors. After his death and cremation, half of his ashes were buried in the Pantheon of Greats in Yerevan, Armenia, with the rest buried in Fresno.

ALEXANDER TAMANIAN (1878–1936) Tamanian was born in the Russian city of Krasnodar. He studied architecture at the Saint Petersburg Academy of Arts. He designed numerous buildings in Russia before moving to Yerevan in 1923. In Yerevan, he took charge of redesigning and modernizing the city to reflect its standing as an important Soviet capital. His design included Republic Square, the Yerevan Opera House, and other impressive structures. Tamanian is buried with other famous Armenians at the Pantheon of Greats in Yerevan. His portrait appeared on the 500-dram note.

FIELD OF KHACHKARS This site near the city of Noratus holds approximately nine hundred khachkars—the largest collection of these "cross stones" in Armenia. Many of the stones serve as grave markers, while others commemorate events.

GARNI TEMPLE This temple at Garni was built in the first or second century A.D. It is the only building in Armenia from the Greco-Roman era. The building was either a temple to a pre-Christian god or the tomb of a Roman-era ruler. The temple is part of a larger archaeological site that contains ancient structures, inscriptions, stone carvings, mosaics (images created with tiny colored tiles), and ruins.

GEGHARD MONASTERY This monastery near Garni sits in a steep canyon. Some of the buildings, including chapels and burial chambers, are carved right into the canyon's rock walls. The monastery has two main churches, both dating from the 1200s. The churches feature dramatic arches and intricate stone carvings.

LAKE SEVAN This large lake has a dazzling blue color that changes with the weather and time of day. The area around the lake has been declared a national park. People come here to boat, swim, fish, and view the abundant wildlife and historic sites.

SELIM CARAVANSERAI This well-preserved structure south of Martuni was built in 1332. It once served as an inn for merchants traveling to, from, and through Armenia. The building offered shelter for both human travelers and their animals.

TSOPK WATERFALL Armenia's rivers feature many waterfalls, including this magical cascade on the Arpa River. The falls are located near the resort town of Jermuk.

UGHTASAR PETROGLYPHS On top of Ughtasar Mountain, more than two thousand petroglyphs are scattered over several square miles. Some carvings show deer, wild goats, snakes, and the ancestors of modern-day cattle. Others show humans hunting and dancing. Archaeologists think the petroglyphs here are between four thousand and twelve thousand years old.

YEREVAN Armenia's capital city has history and art museums, libraries, parks, shops, and monuments. Although it is located in Turkey, Mount Ararat looms above the city. The most moving site in Yerevan is the Genocide Memorial Museum, which honors the 1.5 million Armenians killed by the Turks during World War I.

archaeologist: a scientist who studies the remains of past human cultures

Bible: books of ancient writings that are sacred in the Jewish and Christian religions

blockade: to punish an enemy nation by preventing the movement of goods and people across its borders

communism: a political system in which the government owns and controls all business, property, and economic activity

corruption: widespread dishonesty, bribery, and other illegal activity in government or business

democracy: a form of government in which citizens vote for their own leaders. Most democratic governments guarantee people freedom of speech, freedom of religion, and other basic rights.

diaspora: a community of people who have settled in many different places, far from their ancestral homeland

dissent: opposition to a government or its policies

folk: relating to the music, stories, crafts, and other traditions of the common people

genocide: the deliberate and systematic killing of a racial, political, or cultural group

gross domestic product (GDP): the measure of all goods and services produced in a nation in one year

hydroelectricity: electricity produced by the power of rushing water. People often dam rivers to create hydroelectric power stations.

irrigation: a system of pumps, channels, and other devices used to carry water to crops

khachkars: stones carved with crosses as memorials to honor people and events

nationalism: a philosophy that emphasizes loyalty to one's own nation above all else. Nationalist goals often include independence from foreign rule.

patriarchy: a society in which the father is the head of the household and in which men hold more power than women and children

petroglyph: a carving or inscription on rock

subsistence farming: growing only enough food to feed one's family, with little or none left over to sell

Western: European or North American in outlook, culture, and tradition

"Background Note: Armenia." *U.S. Department of State, Bureau of European and Eurasian Affairs.* **June 2007.**
http://www.state.gov/r/pa/ei/bgn/5275.htm
(April 18, 2008)

This U.S. State Department site provides a wealth of statistics and information on Armenia. Some sections explore politics and foreign relations, including the Nagorno-Karabakh conflict. Other discussions focus on economic development and efforts to strengthen democratic institutions in Armenia. Facts and statistics on history, government, the environment, and society are also included.

"Country Profile: Armenia." *BBC News.* **February 21, 2008.**
http://news.bbc.co.uk/2/hi/europe/country_profiles/1108052.stm
(April 18, 2008)

At this web address, the respected British Broadcasting Corporation provides a comprehensive overview of Armenian history, politics, and media. The site includes fast facts, a timeline of historic events, political discussions, and links to BBC articles and outside websites.

"Country Report: Armenia." *Freedom House.* **2006.**
http://www.freedomhouse.org/template.cfm?page=22&country=7126
(April 18, 2008)

Freedom House attempts to promote democracy and humans rights around the world. It evaluates freedom of speech, elections, governance systems, and justice systems in various nations. Freedom House gives Armenia mixed reviews in its assessment of democratic practices. It notes that the young nation still needs to improve in the areas of elections, governance, and press freedom.

Curtis, Glenn, ed. *Armenia, Azerbaijan, and Georgia.* **Washington, DC: Federal Research Division, Library of Congress, 1995.**

This book was written shortly after the breakup of the Soviet Union. It devotes one chapter to each of the three former Soviet republics of the Caucasus region. Chapters cover the history, geography, society, culture, and economy of each country. Although some of the material is not current, the historical and geographical information is excellent.

Holding, Nicholas. *Armenia with Nagorno Karabagh.* **Chalfont St. Peter, UK: Bradt Travel Guides, 2006.**

This guidebook for travelers offers a thorough picture of Armenian life and culture. The author explores the nation's history, geography, arts, and society. He also includes a city-by-city and site-by-site guide for visitors, plus practical information about transportation, accommodations, food, and language. One chapter is devoted to the disputed territory of Nagorno-Karabakh. (Spellings of this region vary.)

Images of the Armenian Spirit. **DVD. Directed by Andrew Goldberg. New York: Two Cats Productions, 2003.**

This DVD documentary serves as a guide to Armenian art, society, and history. The filmmakers tell the story of Haik, the legendary father of Armenia, as well as tales of many other heroes and leaders. They chart the nation's history, including the genocide of World War I. The film also explores Armenia's fascinating monasteries, khachkars, and other religious artifacts. Finally, it includes beautiful images of Armenia's mountain scenery.

Selected Bibliography

Kaplan, Robert D. *Eastward to Tartary: Travels in the Balkans, the Middle East, and the Caucasus.* **New York: Vintage Books, 2000.**
This memoir recounts the author's travels through eastern Europe and southwestern Asia. It includes an insightful chapter on Armenia in the wake of independence. The author explores economic despair, the war with Azerbaijan, the aftermath of the 1988 earthquake, and other struggles of Armenians in the 1990s.

Payaslian, Simon. *The History of Armenia.* **New York: Palgrave Macmillan, 2007.**
This thorough history examines the Armenian experience from the first kingdom, Urartu, to the twenty-first century. The author provides extensive coverage of the political, religious, and cultural struggles that forged the Armenian identity. In addition to historic detail, the book includes up-to-date material on modern, independent Armenia.

Plunkett, Richard, and Tom Masters. *Georgia, Armenia, and Azerbaijan.* **Footscray, Victoria, Australia: Lonely Planet Publications, 2004.**
This travel guidebook covers the three nations of Caucasus. The chapter on Armenia offers practical information for travelers, plus details on Armenia's history, landscape, arts, and people. Readers will learn about Yerevan and other cities, as well as historic sites. They will also learn about food, festivals, language, and other highlights of Armenian culture.

Turner, Barry, ed. *The Statesman's Yearbook 2008: The Politics, Cultures and Economics of the World.* **Houndmills, UK: Palgrave MacMillan, 2007.**
This reference book includes articles on the nations of the world. In its examination of Armenia, the writers discuss history, politics, economics, and social institutions. The material includes detailed statistics on communications, health care, education, and trade.

Walker, Christopher J. *Visions of Ararat: Writings on Armenia.* **London: I. B. Tauris, 2005.**
This collection brings together writings on Armenia by historians, travelers, anthropologists, and others—most of them British. The essays explore Armenian history, culture, and relations with the nations of Europe. Several of the pieces provide somber commentary on the Armenian genocide of World War I.

"The World Factbook: Armenia." *Central Intelligence Agency.* **January 2008.**
https://www.cia.gov/library/publications/the-world-factbook/geos/am.html (April 18, 2008) l
This website from the U.S. Central Intelligence Agency is packed with up-to-date statistics about Armenian geography, education, health care, communications, transportation, and government. In addition to the statistics, the site includes discussions of Armenia's history, economy, and international relations.

The Armenian Genocide
http://www.theforgotten.org
This website, sponsored by ABC news, is devoted to the memory of the 1.5 million Armenians killed by the Turks in World War I. The site examines the genocide with words and pictures. It includes stories from survivors.

Armeniapedia: The Online Armenia Encyclopedia
http://www.armeniapedia.org
This website is devoted to all things Armenian—from language and food to history, government, and tourism. The site has recipes, language lessons, biographies of famous Armenians, and much more. As with the well-known Wikipedia website, anyone can contribute to Armeniapedia.

Bagdasarian, Adam. *Forgotten Fire*. New York: Laurel Leaf, 2002.
Bagdasarian based this fictional work on the experiences of his great-uncle, who survived the Armenian genocide during his boyhood. The book tells the story of twelve-year-old Vahan, who witnesses the murder of several family members, endures unspeakable horrors, but manages to escape with his life. *Forgotten Fire* was a National Book Award finalist.

Behnke, Alison. *Cooking the Middle Eastern Way*. Minneapolis: Lerner Publications, 2005.
Armenia is not technically in the Middle East, but its cuisine has much in common with Middle Eastern cooking. This book includes easy-to-follow recipes from Armenia and its Middle Eastern neighbors.

Di Piazza, Francesca. *Turkey in Pictures*. Minneapolis: Twenty-First Century Books, 2005.
Historically and culturally, Armenia is intricately tied in with its neighbor to the west, Turkey. The Turks controlled Armenia for many centuries and carried out the genocide of 1.5 million Armenians during World War I. This book in the Visual Geography Series explores Armenia's powerful neighbor in great detail.

Feldman, Ruth Tenzer. *World War I*. Minneapolis: Twenty-First Century Books, 2004.
On June 28, 1914, Austria's Archduke Franz Ferdinand was assassinated, starting a chain of events that divided the world. What began as a single man's act of rebellion ended in the world's first global war. Armenians fought with the Turkish army in horrific conditions, but religious tension led to the deportation and murder of thousands of Armenians living in Turkey during the war.

Hawkins, Susan Sales. *The Fall of the Soviet Union, 1991*. Hockessin, DE: Mitchell Lane Publishers, 2007.
The end of the Soviet Union was a dramatic event—and one that was welcomed around the world. One by one, the former Soviet republics, including Armenia, declared their independence and set up democratic governments. This book tells how the Soviet Union, once a world superpower, disintegrated in the late 1980s.

Hintz, Martin. *Armenia*. New York: Children's Press, 2004.
This book introduces young readers to the geography, history, and culture of Armenia. Color photographs complement the text.

January, Brendan. *Genocide: Modern Crimes against Humanity.*
Minneapolis: Twenty-First Century Books, 2007.
The Armenian genocide was just one of many horrific genocides of the twentieth century. In this thought-provoking book, January examines genocides in Armenia, Cambodia, Rwanda, Bosnia, and Sudan, as well as the Holocaust (the killing of European Jews during World War II). He looks at the causes, implementation, and consequences of these atrocities and asks what we can learn from them.

Kherdian, David. *The Road from Home: A True Story of Courage,*
Survival and Hope. **New York: HarperTeen, 1995.**
Prior to World War I, the author's mother lived in a loving and prosperous family in Turkish-held Armenia. In 1915 she and her family became victims of the brutal Armenian genocide. This Newberry Honor book tells her story of survival.

King, David. *Azerbaijan.* **New York: Benchmark Books, 2006.**
Armenia and Azerbaijan have tense relations. They went to war over Nagorno-Karabakh in the late 1980s. Twenty-years later, the conflict is still not resolved. This book examines Armenia's neighbor to the east.

Márquez, Herón. *Russia in Pictures.* **Minneapolis: Twenty-First**
Century Books, 2004.
One of the great empires of the world, Russia stretches over eleven time zones and two continents. Armenia surrendered to Russian communists and was a member of the Union of Soviet Socialist Republics (USSR) for almost seventy years. This book in the Visual Geography Series explores the country that shaped modern-day Armenia.

Marshall, Bonnie C. *The Flower of Paradise and Other Armenian*
Folktales. **Westport, CT: Libraries Unlimited, 2007.**
This collection includes about sixty fairytales, myths, and legends from Armenia. These stories shed light on Armenian society—past and present. The book also provides background information on Armenia, including history, recipes, and photos.

Ruggiero, Adriane. *The Ottoman Empire.* **New York: Benchmark**
Books, 2002.
For hundreds of years, the Ottoman Empire dominated the Middle East and surrounding areas. It controlled Armenia and many other small territories. This book examines this powerful empire, including its history and culture.

vgsbooks.com
http://www.vgsbooks.com
Visit vgsbooks.com, the homepage of the Visual Geography Series®. You can get linked to all sorts of useful on-line information, including geographical, historical, demographic, cultural, and economic websites. The vgsbooks.com site is a great resource for late-breaking news and statistics.

Captions for photos appearing on cover and chapter openers:

Cover: Khor Virap Monastery looks across the border of Armenia to Mount Ararat, which lies in Turkey.

pp. 4–5 The Caucasus Mountains cover the entire country of Armenia. The range lies between the Black Sea and the Caspian Sea and crosses territory controlled by Armenia, Azerbaijan, Georgia, and Russia.

pp. 8–9 Mount Aragats is the highest point in Armenia.

pp. 20–21 Archaeologists believe that Karahundj, also known as Zorats Karer, is an astronomical observatory dating to more than 7,500 years ago. It stands northeast of Kajaran, a town in southern Armenia.

pp. 38–39 Music lovers dance and clap their hands at an outdoor concert in Yerevan, the capital of Armenia.

pp. 46–47 Visitors to Geghard Church light candles before beginning to pray. The church in Vagharshapat, Armenia, is part of a monastery complex founded by Saint Gregory the Illuminator.

pp. 60–61 A man cuts corn with a scythe in Bagramian, Armenia.

Photo Acknowledgments

The images in this book are used with the permission of: © Victor Kolpakov/Art Directors, pp. 4-5, 11, 12, 14, 17, 59, 60-61, 62; © XNR Productions, p. 6, 10; © HH/PhotoStock.am, pp. 8-9, 38-39; © age fotostock/SuperStock, pp.13, 49 (bottom), 52; © ZSSD/Minden Pictures, p. 15; © Edward Parker/Art Directors, p. 16; AP Photo/Pool, p. 18; © Atlantide Phototravel/CORBIS, pp. 20-21; The Art Archive/Mechitarista Congregation Venice/Alfredo Dagli Orti, p. 22; © Cameraphoto Arte, Venice/Art Resource, NY, p. 23; © Scala/Art Resource, NY, pp. 24, 51; The Art Archive/Palace of Chihil Soutoun Isfahan/Gianni Dagli Orti, p. 26; The Art Archive/Alfredo Dagli Orti, p. 27; Library of Congress (LC-USW33-024211-C), p. 29; © Hulton Archive/Getty Images, p. 30; © Yevgeny Khaldei/CORBIS, p. 31; © Max Sivaslian/Sygma/CORBIS, p. 34; © Igor Gavrilov/Time & Life Pictures/Getty Images, p. 35; © Bruno Morandi/Robert Harding Picture Library Ltd/Alamy, p. 37; © Bill Wassman/Lonely Planet Images, p. 40; © Cory Langley, pp. 41, 68 (both); © Mangasaryan/Peter Arnold, Inc., p. 42; © Karen Asatryan/PhotoStock.am, p. 43; © M. Torres/Travel-Images.com, p. 44; © Kim Karpeles, p. 45; © Bruno Morandi/Reportage/Getty Images, pp. 46-47; © Fernando Moleres/Panos Pictures, p. 49 (top); © Topham/The Image Works, pp. 53, 55; © Trans-World Photos/SuperStock, p. 54; AP Photo/Petar Petrov, p. 57; AP Photo/Karen Minasian, p. 58; © Martin Shakhbazyan/AFP/Getty Images, p. 63.

Front cover: © DEA/C. SAPPA/De Agostini Picture Library/Getty Images. Back cover: NASA.